LOOSE YOUR MONEY

"Make Money Obey You"

Kim K. Sanders

Unless otherwise indicated, all scripture quotations are taken from the *Kings James Version* of the Bible.

LOOSE YOUR MONEY
Make Money Obey You
ISBN: 978-0-9966222-0-2
Copyright © 2015 Kim K. Sanders

Published by:
Kim K. Sanders International, LLC
P.O. Box 236
Little Rock, AR 72203
www.kimksanders.com

All rights reserved.
Printed in the United States of America.

This material is protected by the United States copyright laws. It is not to be copied or duplicated in whole or in part by any method without the written consent of the publisher.

Table of Contents

ENDORSEMENTS 4

DEDICATION 6

INTRODUCTION 8

CHAPTER 1: The Poverty Mentality 10

CHAPTER 2: The Millionaire Mindset 18

CHAPTER 3: How Bad Do You Want It 29

CHAPTER 4: Decide To Prosper On Purpose 39

CHAPTER 5: Prepare For Prosperity 48

CHAPTER 6: Stay Focused Develop Discipline And Be Consistent 59

CHAPTER 7: Let God Establish A Testimony In You 64

CHAPTER 8: Pray It Through 77

CHAPTER 9: You Can't Stop Me Devil! 93

CHAPTER 10: The Divine Manifestation 105

APPENDIX A: Kim's Money Confession 111

APPENDIX B: Kim's Prosperity Confession 114

ABOUT THE AUTHOR 116

ENDORSEMENTS

In Kim Sanders new book, "Loose Your Money," she gives the readers a clear, concise pathway towards gaining prosperity. For those that do not understand the cycle of poverty and how to rise above it, this book demonstrates the necessary steps we must take in order to walk in the mindset of a millionaire and why it is important to do so. If you want to know how to prepare for prosperity, and maintain it afterwards, read this book, the many principals and confessions will not disappoint you.

Bishop Orrin Pullings, Sr.
United Nations Church International

I believe this book is a must read for both saved and unsaved people. The truths that Kim shares in this book are not limited, addressed nor bound to any one segment of society, any race, color or people group. I declare that this book is a must read for both the wealthy and those who are bound by poverty. Kim's straight forward approach, her candid transparency and the simplicity with which she presents these power truths, will help you make positive changes that will enable you to master your money.

Don't read this book and pass it on or lay it aside. No, read it several times and meditate on it. The Principles of prosperity and biblical confessions that Kim shares in this book are not for her alone. If you will apply them, you will discover that for the first time in your life you are a money master. Money will never master you again because you will learn how to make money OBEY YOU!

I'm Prophet Leonard Ford and I endorse and approve this book.

Prophet Leonard Ford
Reality Of The Gospel World Outreach Ministries, Inc.

Absent your goals or aspirations, secular or spiritual, it will take financial resources to get there. Ostensibly, money really does make the world go 'round. As it is universally necessary, we should endeavor to know how to get it, save it, invest it and cause it to reproduce itself for us and those who will come after us. Kim Sanders has outlined practical, Biblical methods to get what we all need - money. Loose Your Money will position you to create lasting wealth and teach your children to do the same. The lessons are easy to understand and apply. Kim's financial principles are on point!

Hon. Mark D. Leverett
Little Rock District Court Judge

DEDICATION

This book is dedicated to my husband, Ernest Sanders Jr., my children, Trinity Latrice Eubanks and Ernest Sanders III. Thank you for your sacrifices, thank you for believing in me, thank you for your unconditional love and for allowing me to fulfill the will of God for my life. It is our time and our turn!

ACKNOWLEDGEMENT

To The one and only, my Lord and Savior Jesus Christ, the Lover of my soul. Thank You for all the things You have done and have allowed me to accomplish thus far. All the glory belongs to You ONLY Father God!

INTRODUCTION

As a little girl growing up, I always knew that there was something different about me and that I was destined for greatness. Although we had nice things, in all honesty we were really broke.

As a single mother raising two children, I remember my mom struggling all throughout life. As quiet as it is kept, we always lived above our means. Most of the time, we lived with my grandparents, who are now gone to be with the Lord. Although I was oblivious to poverty, I saw it all around me; but at the same time I was exposed to seeing the affluent life because my grandfather worked around a lot of wealthy influential people. Somewhere in my mind I always knew I was designed to live the lifestyle of riches and wealth. I always felt in my heart: "I'm living beneath my privileges, I'm not supposed to live like this, there is something better." There was always something in my heart that couldn't stand to be around poverty or lack.

I never looked down on people who were less fortunate than me, but everything in me knew that poverty was not the life for me. I've always wanted the best for other people, even though I lived in a place of lack. Most of my life I found myself trying to convince others about the beauty of life and all the beautiful things that life had to offer but did not quite know how to possess them for myself.

As I look back over my life growing up, I realize that God shielded me from having a poverty mentality and I finally understand why it grieves my heart to see other people living in bondage to poverty. Little did I know that it would be my assignment to teach people how to position themselves for wealth and make a major difference in the lives of multitudes all around the World!

> ***3 John 2: Beloved, I wish above all things that you prosper and be in good health, even as your soul prospers.***

It is not the will of God for us to be poor, regardless of our upbringing and limitations. Throughout my life I have battled with how to break the back of lack and how to break through the forces of darkness that imprisons our financial freedom. I have finally found the keys to break through the opposition, and all resistance to obtain the prosperity oil, money, wealth and riches that God has predestined for us.

As you progress through this book, I believe that a significant impartation will be transferred from these pages, and into your life that will break every hindrance, remove every setback, cease every delay, and demolish all mental anguish, confusion, and torment.

As I carry the weight of people who are experiencing the pain of poverty and debt, it is my mission to inflict major damage to the kingdom of darkness and obliterate every opposing thought to the word of God concerning wealth, riches, finances and money. It is my desire to expose and overthrow the spirit of deception by communicating and articulating the spirit of truth, so you can be free from the stronghold that binds and hinders.

I know that it is the heart of God and my assignment to impart the mind of God that is clothed in my vocabulary to cause a paradigm shift that will transform the minds of those that can house the prosperity oil being poured out of my vessel. This oil is being poured out right now. I seal every crack and hole that may be in your vessel, and declare that no oil will be wasted. Allow the prosperity oil to penetrate your life. Let it transform your mind, and your soul. I am going to be transparent and share the very principles that I have applied in my own life that have loosed breakthrough in my finances. If you execute these principles, you will experience the same freedom.

CHAPTER 1

The Poverty Mentality

"You Must Passionately Despise Poverty."

A man's pattern of thinking is everything. It determines whether he will succeed or fail; win or lose. The mind is where the battle takes place. If the enemy can win the battle of your mind, he wins. We need to uproot seeds that have been planted so that we can lay a foundation for you to understand what it takes to loose your money. In the process, a lot of mental strongholds will be broken; so, let us talk about the poverty mentality.

The word *mentality* is defined as one's mental capacity or endowment, the set of one's mind, or the view or outlook. It refers to your state of mind; your intelligence. My definition of a person's mentality is a certain type or pattern of thinking. It is a preconceived thought pattern, meaning your thoughts have been framed based on your life's upbringing, circumstances, environment, personal experience or even words spoken into your life. Simply put, it is how you perceive the world around you. For example, words that have been spoken into your soul have become your truth. When a person's mindset is developed by such things, it can be very difficult, but not impossible, to uproot.

I want you to think back, even to when you were a child, on the preconceived thoughts that you had. "Preconceived" means a conception or opinion has been formed beforehand. When you form a preconceived thought pattern, you develop an opinion beforehand on the evidence beforehand. On many occasions, the enemy will plant preconceived seeds into your life at a young age, before you are ever exposed to the spirit of truth. He will impregnate you with thoughts of poverty through words that people speak, whether through your parents, teachers, preachers, uncles, or whoever influenced your life as a child. The enemy can plant seeds of poverty through your circumstances, environment, and personal experiences, but the only thing that opposes what the enemy has planted is the Word of God. Think back and see if you can remember any negative words that were spoken over your life that created a poverty stronghold in your life.

Growing up as child, you may have constantly heard "You know we cannot afford that!" or "That costs too much!" If you have heard these statements spoken during your life, there is a great possibility that you developed a poverty mentality. When such statements are repeatedly spoken into a child's hearing on a regular basis, it creates a preconceived pattern of thinking, resulting in a stronghold of poverty being established.

You may have adopted this pattern of thinking during your childhood and allowed it to follow you throughout your adult life in both your personal experiences and life's circumstances. Eventually, you start to believe it and you end up carrying those words in your spirit and soul. Sometimes you do not even know why you think or act the way you do.

Let us look at some of the words that are associated with poverty. The word *poverty* means a state or condition of having little or no money, goods or means of support. It is also defined as being poor. Some of the synonyms associated with poverty are insufficiency, lack, deficit, bankruptcy, debt, barrenness and depletion. The words *lack, deficit, barrenness, and insufficiency* are also associated with defeat. When you hear those words over and over, they create a negative self-image inside you; therefore, you begin to see yourself as a failure, which creates a defeated mindset. Now, you have framed your world with those words and are only able to produce what you have created in your mind. Why? Because words create images; and images create thoughts and thoughts influence the decisions you make, which affects the actions you manifest.

> ***Proverbs 23:7, "As a man thinketh in his heart, so is he."***

Whether you believe it or not, your mindset can prohibit you from being able to rise above your inadequacies and keep you from being able to break out of the invisible cage and bars of lack, causing you to become inferior to prosperity, intimidated by prosperous people or the prosperity message.

Just in case you are still in denial, let me tell you five ways to identify if you have a poverty mentality.

1. You Are Lack Conscious

Those who have a poverty mentality tend to focus on what they do not have. You tend to focus on lack, instead of being prosperity-conscious. Lack is always on the forefront of your mind. I can tell by simply having a conversation with such a person. They always talk about their lack and how they never have enough.

2. You Focus On What You Cannot Afford

If you are always focusing on what you cannot afford, that is a sign of a poverty mentality. You constantly rehearse the words, "I cannot afford" or "I do not have." Those words dominate your thoughts or vocabulary. Just pay attention to what you say over the next couple of days to see where your focus is.

3. Money Makes You Uncomfortable

When people talk about money it makes you either mad or very uncomfortable, especially if it is an amount of money you have never had. Any conversation about money makes you uneasy and causes you to flinch. I notice on occasions that when I talk about money around certain people, they get uncomfortable. You can see it in their body language and their countenance; their whole demeanor changes. If you are going to have money, you cannot be afraid to talk about it. It has to be a normal conversation inside of you.

4. You Are Cheap

People with a poverty mentality are usually very cheap. They do not like to spend money or pay full price for anything. If you are the type of person who is always looking for what we call a 'hook up," or the cheapest price when you make purchases, instead of looking for quality, nine times out of ten you have a poverty mentality. Have you ever gone shopping and the first thing you do is go straight to the sale rack? Do not get me wrong; I am not saying anything is wrong with a good bargain. However, if you go shopping, and you are always going to the sale rack without even considering paying full price, that's an indication that you have a poverty mentality. Okay here's another example: Have you gone to a restaurant and the first thing you do is look at the right side of the menu before you order? Yeah, you know what I'm talking about. LOL! We've all done it. Or maybe you've gone to buy a car and the first place you go to is the pre-owned lot instead of going to look at new cars. Think about it! What is it that causes you to do that? If you never see yourself paying full price for anything, or feel like you have to always shop at discount places, then you my friend have a poverty mentality.

5. You Don't See The Value In Investing In Yourself

If you are the type of person who does not see the necessity of investing into your personal development and view it as a waste, that is a sure sign of a poverty mentality. A poverty mindset will look at the cost instead of the return on the investment. If you are a person who has a poverty mentality, you do not understand that you are your greatest investment and when you invest into yourself, you are investing to receive a return. You are afraid to take the risk because you cannot see the value of the return being far greater than the investment. For example, my sixteen–year-old son owns his own business. He took his earnings he made from his business and reinvested back into his business so he could get a return on his investment. The awesome thing about that is I did not even have to tell him to do that; he did that on his own. His mentality was, "that is just common sense."

Most people are generally afraid to invest because they do not understand their value. It goes right back to how they view themselves, which proves a poor self-image needs to be uprooted in order to walk in prosperity.

Kim K. Sanders

God Wants You To Prosper

Poverty does not come from God. God has a plan for your life and that is to prosper you.

Jeremiah 29:11, "...I know the thoughts that I think toward you, saith the Lord, thoughts of peace, and not of evil, to give you an expected end."

That word, "peace", means prosperity. God desires to overwhelm your life and thoughts with prosperity.

Poverty and prosperity travel in two different directions. They cannot travel the same road. You cannot have prosperity in your life with a poverty mentality. The two do not mix because they produce different fruit.

According to Galatians 3:13, Christ has redeemed us from the curse of the law, having been made a curse for us. Poverty is associated with a curse. In Galatians 3:14, God made a way out for us through the blessing of Abraham, through the Lord Jesus Christ. Having a poverty mentality is a pattern of thinking that opposes the Word of God. It sets up and creates a stronghold in our lives. We must cast down every thought, every imagination, everything that contradicts God's word concerning wealth and prosperity. God is the one who gives us the power or ability to get wealth (Deuteronomy 8:18).

Did you know that God delights in your prosperity? I want you to look at Psalm 35:27 and put your own name in it. You have got to personalize and own it for yourself. The next time you have thoughts of lack and insufficiency, remind yourself that God delights in your prosperity, and He desires that you prosper. You must never determine your ability to prosper by looking at your past experiences or present circumstances.

There are spiritual and practical principles that one must apply to obtain prosperity, and it starts with your thinking. God wants your mind to flourish. He wants your mind to thrive. He wants your mind to bear fruit and to multiply. In order for that to happen, you are going to have to get rid of the poverty mentality. Rid your vocabulary of the words *"I do not have enough," "I do not make enough"* and *"I cannot afford it."* Take your focus off of being lack-conscious, and replace it with being prosperity-conscious. Do not even attempt to pour this new wine into an old bottle. The bible warns us against such practices in Mark 2:22. In order for you to bear new fruit and see the manifestation of your money being loosed, you need to uproot all negative thoughts of poverty and shift your thinking.

I want to teach you how to birth authentic prosperity, loose your money and make money obey you. I will walk you through every principle that I have applied to attract money in my life. The same effort and energy it takes to accept poverty and lack is the same effort that is required to accept and pursue prosperity.

I Am Allergic To Poverty And Being Broke

The very first principle I want to give you is you must despise poverty. Everything inside you must hate poverty. For example, everything in me detests poverty. I hate everything about it. There is nothing good about poverty. I do not know why anybody would believe that God wants them to be poor. What kind of Father would want his children to be poor and live in poverty?

If you look at the synonym for the word "despise", you will see *"allergic to."* I am allergic to poverty and being broke. You have to literally be allergic to poverty. Everything on the inside of you must detest, refuse, and reject everything that is associated with poverty and lack.

I used to be a cosmetologist, and I remember wearing color in my hair. I literally tried every color that you can name. I have been up and down the color chart. After my second pregnancy with my son, I noticed there were chemical changes in my body. If I attempted to put color in my hair, I would have allergic reactions that caused me to breakout into hives. There was one occasion where I used a particular color in my hair, and ended up going to the doctor to get a shot. The doctor told me I had an allergic reaction to something that was in the ingredients of the color dye. Was it the color, you might ask? No, there was something inside me that literally rejected that color that caused me to have a breakout. That is the way we have to handle poverty. You need to have an allergic reaction and breakout to poverty, and all the fruit that goes with it, if you intend to be prosperous and get your money. It is not normal to be broke when you are a child of the King and understand that prosperity is a part of your covenant.

Disassociate yourself from poverty thinking and poverty conversations, so your mind can be renewed to receive prosperity.

> ***Romans 12:2, "And be not conformed to this world, but be ye transformed by the renewing of your mind, that ye may prove what is that good, and acceptable, and perfect, will of God.***

Changing your old thoughts and habits concerning money and the way you are used to operating is a necessity in order to loose money.

One of the questions you need to ask yourself to locate your present mindset is, "Are you afraid of money?" The truth is, if you are afraid of money, you will never have it. You cannot be afraid of money and control it at the same time. If you are afraid of money, that fear means money is controlling you. In essence, you are allowing money to dominate your life.

> ***2 Timothy 1:7, "God has not given you a spirit of fear, but of power, love and a sound mind."***

Fear is an enemy to prosperity and abundance. God never designed for money to control you or your thoughts. If you are going fulfill the will of God for your life, you must conquer the spirit of fear and realize that you must be in control of money and cannot be afraid to think big. You have the power and authority within to loose money and make it obey you.

I want you to declare this affirmation out loud:

Loose Your Money – Make Money Obey You

"I refuse poverty. I reject poverty and everything with poverty. Poverty is not my friend; and it no longer serves me. Therefore, I loose it and let it go. I break all ties with poverty and the spirit of poverty. I curse poverty at the root. Poverty, I disassociate myself with you. I renounce you and all of your fruit. You no longer control me. You no longer have a hold on me. Poverty, you are a curse and I detest you. I set myself apart from you; and I will no longer entertain you. I will no longer allow you to contaminate my thoughts. I eradicate all emotional ties associated with poverty. I decree that all of the roots of poverty in my life are permanently dissolved. I declare my immediate release right now. I receive total liberty in the name of Jesus. I make a choice to covenant with prosperity. And I will adopt prosperous thoughts. I decree and declare that prosperity will fill my mind from this day forward, in Jesus name. Amen."

CHAPTER 2

The Millionaire Mindset

"You Must Believe In Yourself And Know Your Value."

If you are going to loose money in your life, you are going to have to think like a millionaire. Millionaires have success thoughts and a successful pattern of thinking. There is no way that you can loose money into your life without having a millionaire mindset. Becoming a millionaire begins in your mind before you actually become one.

One of the first secrets I have learned about having a millionaire mindset and making money is to be totally responsible for creating my own success. It is nobody else's responsibility to prosper me but me, not even God's.

"But remember the Lord your God, for it is he who gives you the ability to produce wealth, and so confirms his covenant, which he swore to your ancestors, as it is today." (Deuteronomy 8:18 – NIV)

You must realize that God gave you the ability to create and produce wealth. He has placed that ability on the inside of every person on this earth. But it is up to you to tap into that power within and make your own way prosperous and cause good success to come into your life as the scripture says in Joshua 1:8. You already possess all you need to succeed.

So many people in life blame other people for their lack of success. When you shift the blame and do not take responsibility for choices that you have made in life, you give away your power and ability to prosper. The fact of the matter is if you are broke, it is your fault.

Loose Your Money – Make Money Obey You

I had to ask myself this question years ago, "Why am I broke?" It was not until I took full responsibility for my lack of success that things began to shift for me. It caused me to dig deep inside to see what was really going on in my life. I had nice material things, but I was still broke. To be honest, I did not realize I could have the type of success that I always desired outside of my husband. Although I felt like I was supposed to be successful and I had entrepreneurship skills on the inside of me, I did not know how to make it happen. I just knew that I was very unhappy with my life, and I always felt unfulfilled because I knew I was not living in my full potential.

I remember years ago when God and I had this conversation about why I was broke. I cried for weeks because my spirit had been awakened to the fact that here I am 40 years old, a former business owner with no job and now I realize that I am really, really broke. I had no money in savings, no life insurance, no inheritance for my children and no plan for prosperity. I asked myself. "What the heck have I been doing all these years?" Although I had been self-employed the majority of my life, the truth is I did not really know anything about being a successful entrepreneur. The devil relentlessly tried to convince me that I was nothing more than a house wife and mom. Although nothing is wrong with being a housewife and mom, I knew, deep inside, I was more than just that. I always knew I was a visionary with many hidden gifts and talents, but it is so easy to lose yourself, your identity and who God made you to be. People may observe from the outside and immediately assume you are successful, when that assumption can be far from the truth.

The one thing that I was sure of was the call of God on my life to preach the gospel. I was deep in debt, but knew in my heart that I had a mandate to set the captives free from the bondage of debt. At that point I began to ask God "how is this going to happen and what do I do?" I was puzzled because most preachers I personally knew were broke; therefore, I had no one to pattern myself after because I did not want to be like or look like them. Next, I asked God "Lord how in the world can someone have the power to help somebody else when his/her own life looks raggedy?" So I told God that He was going to have to show me what I needed to do, because I refuse to be like most of the preachers I see. I wanted *"Authentic Prosperity"* in my life, which brings me to my next point.

I Only Eat Authentic Prosperity Food

God began to teach me how to adopt a millionaire mindset and birth authentic prosperity. It first started with renewing my mind and planting new seeds. I diligently fed my spirit wealth and prosperity food. Divine revelation began to flow into the hard drive of my spirit man from Holy Spirit. It cost me many years of consistent study and prayer with fasting. God began to connect me with multi-millionaires, and I duplicated their habits and work ethics quietly behind the scenes.

As I continued in my journey to prosperity, my mind was bombarded with questions because there was still a void. I did not quite understand how all this prosperity stuff applied to me. I was asking myself, "okay, I hear all this, and I believe all this, but how in the world is this going to happen for me?" "Could this really happen for me?" "I've wasted so many years of my life and made so many mistakes and bad decisions, what could I possibly do to make this kind of money and attract this type of success in my life?" "How can I have this type of prosperity and still be called to preach?" "Can men and women of God be in business and still preach?" I knew the kind of wealth I was predestined to acquire was not going to come through preaching; therefore, I knew there had to be a connection to the anointing to prosper in business.

Even though my mindset was changing, my circumstances remained the same. God eventually answered my questions and spoke to me saying, "You must believe in yourself and know your value, which is the second principle and secret that I will share with you.

Loose Your Money – Make Money Obey You

Know Your Value

When my husband was running for judge a few years ago, we attended a lot of different functions. I was always by his side, and the first thing people would ask me is, "What do you do for a living?" I felt intimidated and embarrassed to tell people what I did, because I did not want people to laugh at me. So I would tell people I am a stay at home mom until one day God said, "No, that's not what you do, that's who you are. Yes you are a mother and a wife, but you are also a preacher, you are an entrepreneur, you are a mentor." God sees us differently than the way we see ourselves and the way other people see us. Many times we allow people and society to define who we are by what we do, or by our career. What we do is a byproduct of who we are. What you do is not who you really are.

When you understand your value and what you have to offer, and contribute in the lives of others, then you will understand what you do, because who you are is not what you do. For example, now when people ask me what I do, I do not answer them by giving them a title; my current response would be, "I teach leaders practical and spiritual principles to acquire and maintain extraordinary wealth, health and relationships." Now, that is only a part of what I do. A personal development expert to leaders, a breakthrough life coach, a mentor, a minister, an entrepreneur and a published author are who I am.

You are not just one person, but one person with many gifts. When I tell people I can help them produce breakthrough results in their personal, spiritual, and financial life, they want to know more about who I am. So from this day forward, when people ask you what do you do, do not answer them by telling them who you are; answer them by giving them your value. When you understand your divine purpose and what value you add to the world, you are unstoppable. Nothing and nobody can ever take that away from you, no matter what. I remember when I was afraid to open my mouth and tell people anything about myself because I thought they would belittle me. Why? Because I did not understand my value. Now, when I walk into any type of function or atmosphere, I am no longer intimidated because I understand the value that I bring into that place.

People who have a millionaire mentality understand their self-worth and what value they bring into the world. Let us look at the definition of "value" according to dictionary.com.

Value is the worth of something in terms of the amount of other things for which it can be exchanged or in terms of some medium of exchange; it is the estimated or assigned worth; Valuation is monetary or material worth, as in commerce or trade; to consider with respect to worth, excellence, usefulness, or importance; to regard or esteem highly:

When you have something of great value, you will cherish, respect and esteem it highly. When you value something you will also protect it.

To protect means to defend or guard from attack, invasion, loss, annoyance, or insult. It also means to cover or shield from injury or danger.

You must protect yourself from any and every thing that attacks, insults, and challenges who God says you are. Wow! Now that's a revelation! That is why you have to be careful who you allow yourself to be around. There are times when you will have to protect and guard the anointing on your life. I believe that you can come to a place in your life where God will even protect His own investment in you. That is why God will separate you from people who possess a mentality that is a threat to you fulfilling the will of God for your life.

Loose Your Money – Make Money Obey You

If you occupy and entertain the company of people who consistently insult you and superimpose their negative opinions, or thoughts upon you, it is like poison invading your mind, and it will contaminate you. Beware of dream killers and naysayers sent to devalue your worth. Never feel like you have to explain or apologize for guarding and protecting your investment and the anointing on your life.

Your Value Should Be Exchanged For Money

When you understand your value, you understand that an exchange will take place. You are giving your value into the life of someone else in exchange for money. People will pay you for your years of knowledge and expertise. They are paying you for your experience, wisdom, research over the years, and even your mistakes. When you understand your value, you will not have a problem putting a price tag on your services, products, classes, or whatever you are offering.

My husband went to school for several years to be an attorney. As a matter of fact, he has two degrees and has paid a great price for his knowledge in years, and in money; therefore, the return on his investment should be greater. I would say that my husband is quite valuable and comes highly recommended by many people. He does not advertise or market his business, nor does he have a website. For the sake of this example I'd like to compare my husband to a Bentley. Have you ever seen an advertisement or commercial for a Bentley? No, you probably have not. Why not? Because the company understands its value and the name Bentley speaks for itself. Anyone who has ever purchased a Bentley has paid a high dollar price, simply because of its name and value.

In my husband's practice of law, he has a right to charge a high-dollar for his prices, if he so desires, because of his worth. His prices are not based on what he thinks other people can afford but on what he is worth and the value he brings to serve others. Additionally, his reputation speaks for itself. If he did not believe in himself, he would undervalue what he has to offer. If a person may not be able to afford my husband's services, does that mean he is supposed to lower his prices? No, not everyone can afford a private attorney; therefore, they would either get a public defender or represent themselves. You get the picture?

Let's look at a ten of my personal success secrets to a millionaire mindset. These are valuable golden nuggets that I have learned and applied in my life over the years. God never allows me to teach anything to anybody that I have not birthed in my life. These are not things that I've researched on the internet; this revelation knowledge comes from principles for which I have labored and by which I have lived.

1. Invest In Yourself

The proof of believing in you is investing in yourself. Millionaires understand the power of investing. One of the fastest ways to create wealth is to invest in personal development. When investing into your personal development, never look at the cost but rather look at the return on the investment. Every successful person in life understands that they are their greatest investment. No dollar amount should be too expensive when it comes to you. How can you expect others to invest into you, or invest into your business and spend money with you, when you do not have a mindset to spend money and invest into yourself? I understand that if people are going to exchange money with me or invest in my business, I must first invest in myself.

2. Perfect Your Skills And Master Your Craft

In this day and time with everyone competing in business, it is not enough to be an expert in your field; you have to be "the" expert. Learn how to become the master of your craft by perfecting your skills on a regular basis. Perfecting your skills will require you to stay on the cutting edge and will most often pull you out of your comfort zone. One of the ways to perfect your skill is by increasing your mental capacity to receive more.

3. Increase Your Mental Capital

When you are lacking financially or in any other area of your life, it is always because of something you do not know. Always increase your mental capital. Your mental capital is what you know; it is your knowledge, wisdom and revelation. Increasing your mental capital means enlarging your capacity to receive more in order to increase your value, your production, your means and capabilities. Increasing your mental capacity allows you to deliver more to the world. Begin to study income-producing activities in your field of expertise. People will pay you more if you are worth more. Make a conscious decision to do something every day to increase your worth.

4. Invest In A Mentor

Every successful person in life has a mentor or coach. Think about athletes and even celebrities. Everyone who has ever produced success, or millionaire status in life, has a coach or a mentor. Study people you know who are successful in your field and study what it is that makes them successful. In other words, study the mindset of success or the success of your niche.

When you invest into mentors and tap into their knowledge, you are tapping into their cash flow; you are tapping another person's source until it generates cash flow back to you. As a matter of fact, you are tapping into my cash flow right now. If you apply what I am teaching you, it is going to generate in return, a greater investment and a greater cash flow back into your life. How powerful is that? Find your divine connection or mentor and stay connected.

5. Grow Your Ability To Contribute More

If you grow your ability to contribute more, you can command more. This principle relates back to why it is so critical to increase your mental capital. If you have the ability to contribute to where the exchange is more valuable, then you will get more from the flow. More value equals more cash flow.

6. Challenge Your Belief System

How long it takes for you to increase in wealth is determined by your knowledge and what's already in you. Increasing in wealth is based on what has to be eliminated from your life and what must be deposited in you. The first step to making any change is to review your belief system. Begin to challenge every belief system that no longer serves you and is standing in the way of you achieving your dreams and goals. Ask yourself, "Why have I been operating like this?" Next, ask yourself, "What is my relationship with money and what do I really believe about money?"

You must eliminate all conflicting and opposing beliefs that can stand in the way of you producing wealth. Look at every area of your life that is not producing fruit, make a list of those areas and trace it back to the root of a belief system. Remember, you are responsible for your success and you are responsible for your failure.

Loose Your Money – Make Money Obey You

7. Spend On Assets

Spend on assets that give you more in return. As I said earlier, you are your greatest asset; therefore, when you invest into yourself you will see a greater return. It has been stated that rich people acquire assets, things that pay more. Middle class people acquire liabilities, things that cost more and poor people acquire junk, things that have no value.

To acquire the ability to get more cash flow, you must stop acquiring liabilities and start developing assets.

8. Time Is Money

I know you have heard the old saying, "Time is money," right? Well it really is true. If you are going to be business savvy, it is important to understand this. Successful people leverage their time by setting up systems. If you look at most successful people, you will see that they have systems already put in place to generate residual income; they do the work one time and get paid on it over and over again because they understand how to leverage their time. I have several systems already put in place, which allow me to make money while I sleep.

9. Successful People Attract Money

I remember a conversation I had with my husband a few years ago. We were talking about people who chase money and the fact they will do just about anything to make money. I will never forget something very profound he told me. He said, "I don't chase money; money comes to me." And when I thought about it, he was right.

Successful entrepreneurs who know their value and target audience do not spend their time begging, trying to convince people to buy what they have to offer. Successful people spend their time creating solutions to problems, and those solutions attract money like a magnet. One of the most powerful revelations that God taught me is this: "When you chase money, it means that your need for money supersedes your ability to attract money." God never designed you to chase money but rather to be a money magnet. We will talk a little more about this in chapter ten.

10. Successful People Do Not Make Excuses

A part of having a millionaire mindset is understanding that successful people do not make excuses. People who are not successful do what they can; but people who are successful, do whatever it takes. If you are not successful, it is because you are just doing what you can. If you want it bad enough, you are going to do whatever it takes, and your actions are going to come in alignment with what you believe.

The divine manifestation that shows up in your life is determined by your mindset. How you think and view money is critical because it affects how you produce. My question to you is, "how bad do you really want it?" Change your mind, and you will change your life.

CHAPTER 3

How Bad Do You Want It

"You Must Be Obsessed With What It Takes To Produce Wealth And Loose Your Money."

How bad do you want it? This question is a game changer. This question will determine whether you will actually loose your money. Are you willing to do what it takes to produce success or to loose your money? I talk to so many people who tell me they want success but yet their actions do not align with their mouths. I see it a lot in business, especially with people who join network marketing companies. My question is always, "How bad do you really want it?"

When you decide that you really want success, and you are ready for your money to be loosed, the first thing you will say is "Enough is enough. I am willing to do whatever it takes to produce success." The real difference between people who succeed, and those who fail, is the actions of the successful will always line up with what comes out of their mouths.

First, you need to make that decision. It is a natural, conscious, intelligent decision that you want this more than anything. You decide you want to prosper. Prosperity is a decision. And decisions are not based upon a feeling. I can pretty much tell if a person is serious about making money just by looking at his/her daily activities. What you do every day will determine the level of success you will produce.

Are you willing to make the sacrifices that it is going to take to prosper? There is a price to pay for success, which is why so many people are not successful. Most people are not willing to pay the price, which, believe me, can be quite expensive.

One thing I have learned on this journey to success is that in order to eat the bread of success, you must be obsessed with doing what it takes to produce success. Notice I did not say that you must be obsessed with success or that you must be obsessed with money. You must be obsessed with *"doing what it takes"* to produce success.

The word "obsessed" means to think about something unceasingly or persistently, to dominate or preoccupy the thoughts, feelings or desires of.

Just take a moment to really think about what you desire. What is persistently preoccupying and dominating your daily thoughts? If you are going to be successful, you must be obsessed with what it takes to produce those things.

Let us look at ten principles you must be obsessed with in order to loose money and produce success.

Principle #1. Make Up Your Mind

You must have a made-up mind. Nothing, or nobody, should be able to sway you or change your mind. You cannot be double-minded. When you decide that you are tired, and enough is enough, you will become obsessed with having a made up mind. You will set your face like a flint, or hard stone. In other words, you will not be moved. It does not matter what comes your way, you will establish your heart to have a made-up mind. So, when the storms and blizzards of life come, your mind is set. Nothing can stop you! You will hold fast to getting your money. You will have the tenacity of a bulldog.

Loose Your Money – Make Money Obey You

Principle #2. Believe You Deserve It

This is directly related to value and knowing your worth. Everything revolves around what you have to give. Everything on the inside of you must believe that you deserve to be prosperous. It is not up to anybody else but you. If you do not believe in yourself, then you will not believe that you are worthy of what is to come. You must be obsessed with believing that you deserve to be wealthy.

Principle #3. You Must Have A Strong Desire For Prosperity

There must be a strong, overwhelming desire on the inside of you to be prosperous. I will use myself as an example because my desire to prosper goes beyond and deeper than me wanting to have money. I know that I have an assignment and a mission to help other people get their money; therefore, I must be an example of total life prosperity. I literally see your money being loosed, along with thousands of other people.

I literally sit and visualize myself changing the lives of thousands. I am obsessed with the desire to change lives. It is now a part of my DNA. It has to become a part of your daily thoughts. It must become a part of who you are. I think success; I breathe success; I live success. Do not be afraid to dream big. The sky is the limit. If you can see it, it can happen.

Principle #4. Develop Vision

You have got to see it. See yourself rich. See yourself prospering. See your money loosed. Be obsessed with seeing it. If you can see it, it is yours.

God does not give ideas, insight, and concepts for them to stay in your mind. If you are a visionary, it is because God puts the vision inside you so you can see it before it manifests. Why do you think you keep seeing it? God gave you a powerful imagination. Images are very powerful. That is why you have to be careful what you allow to go before your eyes. You have the ability to create what you see. Do not depend on others.

Many people have vision boards. I have a vision board. For my vision board, I did not go cut out pictures from a magazine; I created what I saw. God will always allow you to see what is possible. You just need to know how to tap into it to receive it. You may be saying, "You mean to tell me, that God is allowing me to visualize something I don't have and it's possible for me to have it?" Absolutely. I have done it many times.

Principle #5. Eat The Bread Of Success

You must be obsessed with eating the bread of success. In essence, you have to feed yourself the very thing you are trying to produce. Taste it, chew it, and savor the taste. Feed yourself success. If you want it bad enough, you must eat the bread of success. You need to be eating money food. In other words, you need to be reading success books, like this book. Feed the desire until it becomes so strong on the inside of you, it cannot help but to produce. These are things that people do when they want it bad enough. If you are not doing these things, then you need to start.

The more you feed yourself money food, the more you are building yourself up and the more you solidify the image of success in your mind. Eventually, it will pay off.

Loose Your Money – Make Money Obey You

Principle #6. Prioritize Properly

I see so many people who look at other people and wonder why they are successful. It is because successful people understand how to prioritize properly. When I talk to people and they tell me how badly they want success, but they are not making their success a priority, I tell them, "You don't want it bad enough." Prioritizing means putting your success first and being obsessed with the necessary things it takes to produce the manifestation of success. Many times people have their priorities out of order. It is sad because sometimes we look for success in so many different things and we miss it. You cannot neglect the steps and principles that I am giving you. Everybody wants the get rich quick formula. There is no get rich quick formula.

When you are building wealth or a business, material things cannot be the forefront of your focus. You have to make some sacrifices until you are in a position to buy those things with no sorrow added. Material things should not be a priority. Sometimes we feel like we are missing out because we compare ourselves to what other people have and are doing and therefore attempt to keep up with the Joneses. I mean, who are the Joneses anyway? I am still yet to meet them.

I do not know what it is you need to prioritize in your life, but I challenge you to look at the things that are in your life and see if it is bringing you any closer to your desire. See if it is bringing you any closer to the success that you desire. What are the irrelevant things that need to be eliminated in your life? Is it serving you? Is it just a good thing to do or is it a God thing to do?

You cannot allow other people to dictate what they think you should be doing. When I put my success at the forefront of my future, I follow God's instructions of how I should prioritize things in my life. After all, it is my life. For years, I allowed what other people thought

I should be doing to dictate my priorities, until I woke up one morning and realized, "you know what, I'm taking authority over my life, over my finances and I'm going to make it happen for myself." My desire to be successful was so strong that I was willing to risk people thinking whatever they wanted to think about me, to go after everything that God said I could have. I have spent many days and nights wondering why people who have the ability to help me advance in life would not do so. Then one day I had a spiritual awakening to never again in life worry about those who will not help me. My priority had become to position myself to help others succeed.

I sacrificed for a short time many things that I may have wanted only so that I could have a lifetime of success. The sacrifices I made were temporary so that I can enjoy life to the fullest, living a maximized life. When everybody else was going out, having a good time, spending money on vacations, I was working, building my wealth. If you want it really bad enough, you will become obsessed with prioritizing properly.

Principle #7. Leave Your Comfort Zone

You have got to be obsessed with coming out of your comfort zone. Right here is where a lot of people do not make it. Most people do not want to come out of their place of comfort to do things they have never done because they do not want to be stretched. Coming out of your comfort zone requires you to be stretched. The good news is a mind that is stretched can never go back to its original capacity. Once you learn something, nobody can ever take that away from you.

When you start to tap into a new industry, you will come out of your comfort zone because you are depositing new seeds in your spirit. It may even feel like starting at the bottom when you are doing something that you have never done. But it is worth it.

In my Business Breakthrough Boot Camp, I train people to set up automated systems and how to make automated income. In other words, I teach people how to make money while they sleep. I teach people internet marketing and how to build an online business. There is a lot of deep stuff that goes into learning internet marketing. There is a learning curve, especially if you do not know anything about internet marketing. It has taken me years to learn the things that I know now, and I am still learning. There is a science to internet marketing that caused me to definitely come out of my comfort zone and be stretched. Sometimes it can be painful being stretched. When I first started my business, I had no one to help me build, which meant a lot of tears, late nights and early mornings. I can truly say the Holy Spirit taught me most of what I know.

Principle #8. Do The Work

You cannot be lazy and make money. You have to do the work. I believe there are things we must do both in the natural and in the spiritual realm in order to produce prosperity and success. I also believe we first have to birth prosperity in the spirit, before it will manifest in the natural. Prayer is an essential key to manifesting prosperity in your life.

I am obsessed with prayer because I know that when I pray, God is going to give me the wisdom and instructions I need to carry out His plan for my success. He is going to give me the know-how and everything that goes along with it. I personally spend a lot of hours in prayer, and as a result, God taught me how to prosper. Spending time with God taught me how to do what I did not know how to do in the natural.

A lot of things I had to learn the hard way because at the time, I could not afford to hire anyone to teach me some of what I am teaching you. I had to figure it out, and pray it through. It cost me a lot of hours of prayer, study, and research. I remember when I first learned about internet marketing and how to build websites. I cannot even begin to tell you how many years of research, reading, and mistakes it took before I even understood what I was doing. I spent countless hours, days and nights building website after website and learning the science of what makes internet marketing work, until I mastered that skill, and there is stuff I'm still learning. My family can always tell when I am working on something because I will have my face set like a flint, focused with a mission not to stop until the project is complete.

Today, we live in a society where everybody wants everything already laid out for them. Grown folks do not want to put in the work it takes to produce success. It just does not happen that way. How do you think you are going to loose your money? Sometimes, people expect you to do the work for them. If you do not do the work, you are not going to produce the success. That's just the bottom line. You have to develop a strong, consistent work ethic, which means you have to be willing to put in the hours necessary. Sometimes, that means doing things you have never done to receive things you have never had. For example, I stopped watching television so I could produce programs and systems that would give me residual income. What are you willing to do differently? Instead of watching TV all evening, or all day, you may have to read. What are your daily activities? What you do every day will determine the life you will have. Your daily activities will determine whether you will stay broke or whether you will produce success in your life.

Loose Your Money – Make Money Obey You

Principle #9. Be Diligent

You have to be diligent in all the above principles. Diligence is what it takes to be successful. You cannot depend on the world's system to prosper you. The world's system was not set up for you to be prosperous or become a millionaire. Think for a moment and see if you can identify anyone who works a nine-to-five job and has become a millionaire by doing so. Millionaires own businesses; they do not work for others, because they are diligently building wealth for themselves.

Principle #10. Be Consistent

Consistency is the key to breakthrough. When you get this revelation, you will not give up, even if what you are doing does not appear to be working. If you consistently tap a solid rock in the same spot with a jack hammer, eventually it will be shattered. See poverty as that solid rock and just keep tapping at it with the principles I have outlined above.

Be consistent, even when no one else is doing so. Never base what you do on what others are doing or by how you feel. Keep on pressing, even if you have to reposition yourself to get it right. I made a lot of mistakes in my business, simply because of ignorance and felt like giving up many times. I often compare my journey to the story of Noah in the Bible. I can only imagine that Noah felt stupid, tired, humiliated, and embarrassed when God told him to build an ark because it was going to rain. Keep in mind, that when God told him to build the ark, Noah had nothing to compare it to. So he had to follow God's detailed instructions. I'm sure there were times of frustration, fear and doubt during this long process. Two things stood out to me in this story: The first was Noah's consistency and the fact that he did not give up nor give in to the pressure of friends and family but, in obedience to God, he stayed true to what he knew. Second, Noah did not give in to his feelings and he kept building the ark, therefore, witnessed the manifestation of rain. Of course there is more to this story, but my point in sharing this is to encourage you to be obsessed with consistency and stay the course as you build your ark of success so that you can witness the rain of prosperity.

CHAPTER 4

Decide To Prosper On Purpose

"You Must Know Your Definite Concrete Purpose."

If you are going to prosper you must make an intelligence conscious decision that you're going to prosper on purpose, it is a choice. If you look at the life of any successful person I guarantee you they all have this one thing in common. This is something that you must settle in your spirit. Wishing and hoping will not bring an abundance of prosperity and money into your life. You don't wish to prosper, you decide to prosper and then once you decide you must plan clearly defined definite fixed ways to acquire prosperity.

In this chapter let's talk about 10 proven ways to prosper on purpose

1. Clearly Define Your Definite Purpose

Everyone has a God given purpose in life, but not everyone's purpose has been clearly defined. The only way you will be truly fulfilled, have authentic peace and live in abundance is by discovering your God ordained definite purpose.

The Word definite means clearly defined or determine, not vague or general, fixed, precise.

There is nothing like being able to serve others knowing your definite purpose. I believe until your purpose has been clearly defined you will never be completely fulfilled in life and will always be searching for purpose. Why do you think people often go back to school after graduating from college? You may think it's because they don't make enough money, but I truly believe it is because they are not fulfilled and they are trying to discover their divine purpose. When you clearly define your God given assignment it will give you the confidence you need in order to prosper on purpose and create the life that you desire.

Here are a few questions to assist you in discovering your divine definite purpose. What is it in life that you absolutely love to do? In other words - what stirs your passion, that thing that you do effortlessly? I'm not talking about what you desire to do but the thing that flows out of you naturally? Make a list of these things and narrow it down to the top three things. I know for me, if I'm not teaching and training somebody I am not fulfilled.

I remember my mother telling me all throughout the years that I love to "fix people." Even as a child, and all throughout high school, I was always the one that everyone came to for advice because I had the boldness to tell people the truth. I was the kid who tried to help solve everyone's problems. Even as an adult I found myself looking at other people's situations, getting frustrated with them for making bad decisions in life, knowing I had the answer to their problem. I remember having such assurance thinking to myself, "If they would just do what I'm telling them to do, then the problem would be solved." Now that I understand my definite purpose, I realize that God put the desire inside of me and the ability to help people with personal development. It is in my DNA to be a problem solver.

Other people will often recognize gifts in you that you may not see in yourself, which leads me to my next question. What do people recognize in you and often come to you for? This may be an indication of what you are called to do. One of the things I have noticed in my 25 plus years of ministry and business is - your divine assignment will automatically and authentically attract your target audience. In order to prosper on purpose, you must know who your target audience is, which means knowing who you are called to serve.

Loose Your Money – Make Money Obey You

Knowing where you bring forth the most fruit and produce extraordinary results plays a critical part in prospering on purpose. Never allow anyone to decide this for you or you will be miserable. It is important to know what you can give 100% of your whole life to doing. Ask yourself, what thoughts, visions, and dreams are impossible to put out of your mind? When you can answer all of the above questions my friend, you have found your reason and passion for living. You will get up every day with a sense of anticipation and meaning because you know you are doing what you were born to do, which will lead you to prosper on purpose.

2. Determine What You Intend To Give

Now that you understand that you must clearly define your definite purpose, you must determine exactly what you intend to give in exchange for the money you desire to make. Now this is very powerful and very critical to understand, because so many people do not have this revelation, especially Church folks. There is no such reality as getting something for nothing. So, what will you offer in exchange for the money that you desire to make? How do you plan to make it? You need to understand there has to be an exchange; it is not going to just happen. I especially want people in the body of Christ to really get this revelation because sometimes we come into the Kingdom of God and we get dumb all of a sudden. It seems like we lose our senses and think that all this abundance of wealth and abundance of money is going to come into our lives automatically with no exchange. It is no different than sowing a seed and receiving a return on that seed. If you don't plant, you won't reap. So it is with prospering on purpose, you must give something in exchange for money. It is foolish to think that you are going to have money without giving anything in exchange.

3. Decide What Vehicle To Use

After determining what you will give in exchange for money, then you must decide what vehicle you will use to make money. The speed at which you desire to travel will determine the vehicle you choose in getting to your desired goal. Although building wealth is a process and I don't believe in get rich quick schemes, you still must decide, do you want to prosper slow or fast? I desire to prosper as fast as possible therefore I chose a vehicle that can accommodate my travel.

If you think about it there only a few vehicles in which you can travel to the road of prosperity. Think about if you were taking a long trip, would you want to take the bus, the train, or would you want to take the airplane? Decide what mode of transportation you want to take and at what speed do you want to travel. Keep in mind that you are in complete control of your destination.

My preferred mode of transport is a Concord Jet. It gets there faster, with no stops in between. It is going to take longer to ride the bus because there are many pit stops. If you ride the train, you may get there a little faster, but you still stop. The airplane is one of the fastest ways to get to a place or destination, even when you have connecting flights or lay overs, it is still going to get you there faster than it would with ground transportation.

You can travel the road to success by working a secular job and trade time for money, which is kind of like riding the bus, it will take a long time to build wealth but eventually you will get there depending upon how much you desire to acquire in life. If you are the type of person who desires to produce massive success then I suggest you think about owning your own business.

Loose Your Money – Make Money Obey You

Being an entrepreneur is like riding the train or plane to the road of prosperity; both will get you to success faster than working a nine to five. If you are going to become an entrepreneur or own your own business think about whether you will offer a service or sell something. Selling your own products is a sure way to build wealth and earn residual income. If you study people who have great success, they either offer a service, have their own products, or they are a distributor selling someone else's products. If people are going to exchange money with you, there has to be something that you are offering that is in high demand or of great value. The first question to ask yourself when deciding if any product is a good fit for your business is, does it align with your divine purpose? Is what you're offering in high demand and will what you're offering change lives?

Direct sales and network marketing is another vehicle to look at that can produce massive success. Many people look at direct sales and network marketing as a negative but I would like to show you some of the advantages I have discovered.

In business, I have used both direct sales and network marketing as vehicles to produce multiple streams of income. Network Marketing and Direct Sales is like the concord jet of business. In my experience I have found both to be one of the fastest ways to build wealth and create residual income. I am not a sales person, nor am I a network marketer, but because I am a business woman and I understand numbers, I have used direct sales and network marketing as vehicles to build seven different streams of income to create residual income.
While many people disrespect the industry of direct sales and network marketing, they do not understand the different characteristics it provides. One of the key things that it teaches is your ability to leverage. It offers you the ability to collaterally come together with like-minded individuals and combine efforts as a group of people to generate income to where you are no longer working for money but

money is now working for you. That my friend, is just common sense and business savvy.

When choosing your vehicle to prosperity you want to make sure it is something you are highly passionate about. It has to be more than just making money because if you are not passionate about it, you will not stick with it. Too many people are just trying to make a quick buck, chasing a dollar. That is why you see people doing all kinds of stuff, jumping from one thing to the next big thing, because they are not passionate about what they are doing.

4. Fix Your Mind On A Specific Amount Of Money You Desire

If you're going to prosper on purpose, you must fix it in your mind the exact amount of money you want to make. Don't settle for, "Oh I just want to make a lot of money." You must be specific and you must be definite. Remember you are prospering on purpose therefore you must count up the cost in advanced. In other words, how much money will it take for you to live the lifestyle you desire and what is your level of living? This is what you have to establish. If you are going to prosper on purpose, everything must be crystal clear and you must be specific. Not everybody has the same vision for prosperity. Not everyone desires to make the same type of money. Not everyone desires the same level of living.

These are questions you need to consider: "Do you like to travel?" "How often do you plan to take vacations?" "Does your lifestyle require shopping?" "Does your lifestyle require giving and if so how much?" "Do you have children?" "Do you plan to finance them through college?" "Do you have an inheritance that you want to leave for your children and grandchildren?" Make sure that when you determine these things, you are not basing your needs off somebody else's or you are not comparing your level of living to anybody else.

Loose Your Money – Make Money Obey You

It is foolish to compare your level of living or your quality of life to someone else because your assignment and purpose in this life will determine your level of living. For example, I am called to teach people how to produce wealth therefore it is going to require that I live a prosperous life in order to be an example of total life prosperity so my lifestyle will be a lot different than the average person.

5. Create A Definite Plan

Once you have determined that fixed amount that it takes to manifest the lifestyle you desire, you must come up with a definite, concrete plan for carrying out your desire. You will need to back your plans with persistence, and consistency because persistence and consistency does not recognize failure, it never quits.

How do I create a concrete definite prosperity plan to prosper on purpose? First of all, you must understand that money is a numbers game. It does not matter what business you are in, whether in business for yourself, or selling a product, you must know the numbers and do the math. For example, if you plan on making $20,000 a month. Let us do the math for $20,000 a month. This can be applied to any amount that you come up with, but for the sake of example, that is $240,000 a year. In order for you to make $20,000 a month, that comes to $5000 a week, which is $1786 daily. You need to figure out what you will offer, how much you will charge, and how many sales you need per day to meet your goal. This tells me that your activity must be in alignment with your desired goal. This will require you to put together a marketing campaign and strategy to coincide with the financial goal that you want to accomplish and have your systems already in place. That my friend, is a definite concrete plan to prosper on purpose.

6. Write Out Your Goals

And the Lord answered me, and said, write the vision, and make it plain upon tables, that he may run that readeth it. (Habakkuk 2:2)

Write a clear, conscious plan in which you will accomplish your goal. You have to write it out so you can see it and have it before you. Write the vision, and make it plain so you can also stay focused.

Write out the amount of money you intend to acquire. Be detailed. It is not enough for it to just stay in your head, for you to think about it. You need to see it on paper. I have my vision written out on paper, on my iPad and journals. I have a strategic, definite, concrete plan; and I continue to update it once I meet my financial goal.

Once you write out how you plan to accomplish your goal, and you are specific, then you need to write out the action it requires for you to produce and maintain the manifestation of your goal. For example, write it out in an affirmation, "I will sell four programs per day." or "I will make contact with 10 people per day." or "I will market 5 times per day." Use the phrase "I Will." These two words are powerful. It means you are taking control, and holding yourself accountable. You are setting the standard when you say those words. You are prophesying your own destiny and future.

7. Make Daily Affirmations

This is important if you are prospering on purpose. When you make your daily affirmations, you are going to read your written statements out loud. Read them at least twice daily. It helps to build an image on the inside of you. It will challenge you to believe in yourself when you read, "I will prosper on purpose." "I will make $20,000 a month." "I will market every day." Keep these affirmations before you.

Loose Your Money – Make Money Obey You

When you get up in the morning and you have your quiet time with God, speak your affirmations out loud before you go to work. Say them again before you go to bed, let it be the last thing on your mind and in your heart. I have included a couple of affirmations at the end of this book for you to speak daily.

8. Establish A Set Date

Establish a set date that you intend to possess the money and start immediately putting your plan into action. Get a goal before you. I have a goal calendar so I can stay on task and be held accountable to do the work. This will challenge your integrity, and your work ethic to see if you are really going to do what you say. That is the difference between successful people and unsuccessful people. Successful people have it before them and they immediately start putting it into action.

9. Do The Work

You got to do the action that is required. You have to put all these principles into action. The problem I see in so many cases is people not doing the work. You cannot be lazy and prosper. Procrastinators don't prosper. Do it now.

10. Position Yourself For Prosperity

You can make the affirmations every day all day, but if you are not properly positioned for wealth you will not receive anything. You must position yourself for prosperity if you're going to see the manifestations of success in your life.

CHAPTER 5

Prepare For Prosperity

"You Must Position Yourself For Wealth."

If you are going to prosper on purpose, you must make the right provisions, by preparing properly for prosperity. You must prepare every part of your life for prosperity. You have to prepare mentally, emotionally, and you must prepare others around you, especially your family. If you are an entrepreneur and you have employees, you want to prepare your employees, and people that work close to you, whether you are in business, or in ministry. You definitely want to prepare the people in your circle of influence because if you are growing and the people around you are not prepared, they won't be able to handle the increase that is coming into your life.

Personally I cannot have just anybody working with me, whether in business or ministry. People who work with me must understand my lifestyle and what it takes for me to produce success. They have to understand how to keep up with my pace and the rhythm of my work flow. I have had many people come and go because they could not handle who I am, and what I do.

A part of preparing for prosperity is learning how to deal with persecution. You need to be prepared mentally and emotionally because much persecution comes with having a lifestyle of abundance. When persecution comes, unfortunately you are going to have people that are jealous. There may be people who feel intimidated by who you are and your future but always stay in a position of humility so God can get the glory.

Loose Your Money – Make Money Obey You

In order to properly position yourself for prosperity there may be some areas of your life that you need to identify that may be causing delays to your success. Some things we talked about in the previous chapters but let's look at some of it in more details. I want to bring to your attention seven reasons why you may not be properly prepared for wealth.

Reason #1. You May Not Know Your Divine Purpose

In chapter four we talked about clearly defining your definite purpose but let's look a little deeper at how your divine purpose relates to prosperity. A part of preparing for prosperity and wealth is recognizing that God placed gifts in your life to prosper you. I believe there are provisions through your gifts. The enemy works overtime trying to deceive and confuse people about who they are, because when you understand the authenticity of who you are, that is when you can add value to the lives of others and as a result prosper.

Proverbs 17:8 says, *"A gift is as a precious stone in the eyes of him that has it."* The very gift that God has placed inside you is precious. It is like a precious stone; like a diamond. The scripture continues, *"…withersoever it turns, it prospereth."* In other words, wherever you turn, it will prosper you. It is important that you understand and know what your gifts are and the value of your gifts, it will bring prosperity into your life.

I remember as a young adult being severely tormented by the enemy concerning my gifts. I always knew I was gifted, but yet he would send people to make me feel bad about the uniqueness of my gifts. Negative seeds were planted in my life to try to make me fearful of using my gifts. The devil would use people to try to shut me down to get me to completely stop using my gifts. As I became mature in the things of God, I came in to the knowledge of how my gifts related to my divine purpose. When I started to operate in my purpose using my gifts, the game changed. That is when the shift began to take place, and the authentic power of God came upon my life.

You should be using your gifts to build wealth. What is driving you? What is that thing that just makes you tick? What do you see yourself doing? What is it that gives you joy? Do you think God would put those burning desires and gifts in you for nothing? Do you think that you are just born to work, pay bills and die? Do you think you are supposed to just go to work every day and be stressed out with your boss and then come home tired and depressed? Is that what you think life is all about? Do you really think God would give you all these gifts and talents to keep serving and working for somebody else to make their dream come true and not yours?

I definitely believe in serving in another man's vision, especially while we are cultivating our gifts. But there comes a time and place in your life when it is time for you to use your gifts to build your own wealth and vision. It is hard to give all of your efforts, energy and full attention to somebody else's dream and vision while trying to fulfill what God has called you to do. If you allow it, other people will keep working you until you are tired, depressed and dead, they don't care. They will work you and give you a low paycheck and high blood pressure. Something is wrong with that. The world's system is not designed for you to prosper.

I want you to think about this and write the answers down. What difference do you desire to make in the world? What did God give you to make a difference? Do you feel like what you're doing right now is a match for your abilities that God has given you? Think about your personality and everything that is in you. Do you know we all have different personalities for a reason? It is part of your purpose. For instance, I am very bold and very straightforward. I cut to the chase and that is a part of who God made me to be. The thing that stands out most about my boldness is the ability to dissect any situation and get straight to the root of the problem, to offer solutions that produces breakthrough results. Knowing who you are and what you have been put on this earth to do to make an impact in somebody else's life will prosper you. Identify a problem, then create a solution to the problem and get paid to fix it. There is money in creating solutions to people's problems. I am creating a solution to your problem right now. When you understand who you are, and how your gifts relate to your divine purpose, you can properly prepare for prosperity. You will be unstoppable and can go after your dreams with full force.

Reason #2. You May Be Stuck In Your Ways

Many people lack success simply because they are stuck in their ways and won't take the time to learn or do anything different. A sure way to tell when someone is stuck in their ways is by having a conversation with them. Have you ever been talking to someone trying to explain something to them and it seems as if what you are saying to them is going in one ear and out the other ear? I can always tell when people are not receiving what I'm saying because there will be such a strong resistance that they are not open to new things. Most times it is because they don't want to do what is necessary to take their business or finances to the next level. They are afraid to come out of their comfort zone. Some people are just like bars of iron when it comes to doing something new. A person who does not want to learn new things is like someone still trying to use cassette tapes in a digital age. Being resistant to new ways of thinking and doing things is a sure way to stay in poverty and lack.

In chapter two we briefly talked about increasing your mental capital and perfecting your skills. Increasing your mental capacity is a major process in preparing for prosperity. One of the main reasons many people lack prosperity is because they will not increase their mental capacity to become more to offer more value. Always be a student, forever learning and implementing what you learn. If you are going to properly prepare for prosperity you must be open and willing to do and learn new things

Reason #3. You May Be Afraid To Step Out Of The Box

A sure way to prepare for prosperity is being willing to come out your comfort zone. You cannot be afraid to step out the box. A lot of people are in lack because of fear. They are afraid of failing and get trapped with the "What If" syndrome. The what if attitude will keep you passive and broke. You cannot be afraid and prosper at the same time. Fear is designed to keep you paralyzed. Do you know how many people sit on ideas and refuse to pursue their dreams because of fear?

Do not be afraid to step out the box. Maybe you are called to do something nobody else has done. If God put it in you to do, do not be afraid to be unique. You do not have to be like everybody else. Personally I have very peculiar gifts in everything that I do – business and ministry. But you know what? I love being me and I love what I do. Outside of that, I do not function well. A couple of my gifts are training, and speaking into the lives of people. I know my approach is very different, but I am not afraid to be me and that is why I produce breakthrough results. I am not afraid to be loud and in your face telling you that you are broke because you are scared. This is my personality and God gave me this. He gave me the boldness to tell you that you are broke because you are stuck in your ways, and you don't want to learn nothing different and do nothing different. I am comfortable in saying that. Not everybody can tell you that and get away with it, but I can. LOL! You got to know your limits.

Loose Your Money – Make Money Obey You

Everybody can't do the same thing. Do not be afraid to step outside the box and be authentic. You are very powerful in your grace; therefore use your gifts with everything in you.

Reason #4. You May Not Be Planning Properly

One of the reasons why you may not be producing success is because you failed to plan. If you are going to prepare for prosperity, you must plan. There is an old saying, "When you fail to plan, you plan to fail." You need a comprehensive game plan.

In football, they have what you call a playbook for the players of the team, and in that playbook is all the plays outlined for each player to do for each play. So, it is like the plan in hope of winning the game. You should have an outline written out to follow so you can know what to do in order to win, in order to prosper on purpose. Then, you must know the necessary required action to fulfill the plan.

Reason #5. You May Not Be Positioned Properly

In preparing for success you must understand timing and positioning. You must position yourself for wealth and prosperity. Now, what do I mean position yourself? When you position yourself, you need to have the right systems in place. For example, I am preparing to take my business to the next level of increase, so I must be prepared for the massive success that is getting ready to hit my business. In order to have massive success, I must have my systems already in place. If I am increasing my audience and sphere of influence, then my systems have to be ready and set in place to accommodate the anticipated audience, so when they come I am set with great expectancy. Here is another example. If I am expecting to sell 100,000 copies of my book, then it is imperative that I have a distribution system already in place.

You must have stuff in order. Get your systems in place and be ready. In other words, position yourself properly.

Reason #6. You May Not Be Sowing Into Fertile Grounds

You need to sow into good ground. I believe in tithes and offerings, but what I am referring to here is sowing seed into your future. I am not just talking about sowing financial seed although that is a prerequisite for prosperity but I am also talking about sowing into you. You are good ground. Are you making the necessary investments? A part of preparing for success and prosperity is preparing your field properly for a great harvest. Preparing requires you to have seed in your spiritual and natural ground.

You have to think like a farmer. Before a farmer goes out to sow seed, he has the desired harvest already in mind that he wants to reap. Based on the harvest that he wants to reap will determine how much seed he takes with him to the field. A farmer always prepares his seed in advance before he goes to the field. How does this apply to finances? You can look at this in a spiritual way and in a natural way. Sow into whoever or whatever it is going to take to get you to your desired result. It could be a mentor, or a class.

Sometimes we lack success because we don't know the right people. Sow into people who can help you. A mentor taught me this; sometimes you have to buy your friends. There are times where you will have to buy into circles of influence. For example, I have invested into businesses, and circles of influence, because it was necessary for me to meet certain people in order to increase in certain areas, why because they had what I needed, so, I bought into it. When you buy into coaching programs or into personal coaching, it gives you an advantage. When people see that you are willing to invest in their trainings, you open the door to new opportunities and build possible connections.

There is a particular person that I bought a training program from a few years ago. It increased both my sphere of influence, and my knowledge base. It also brought about a new relationship. I bought into millionaire programs and it opened the door for me to connect with millionaires. It is very important to connect with the right people in order to be successful. When you buy into circles of influence, favor will often be released. God will cause you to have favor with people, but you have to position yourself and place yourself before them. It may be costly, but it is worth it.

Take your seed and invest it wisely so it can multiply. You must invest in your future based on your desired harvest. Determine what you will invest and where you invest and keep in mind that not every field returns the same harvest, so you must be careful where you sow because after all you will reap what you sow and it will come back into your life.

Reason #7. You May Be Allowing Distractions

Distractions are one of the main strategies the enemy will use to keep you in a place of stagnation and frustration. One of the most powerful lessons I have learned in life and preparing for prosperity is you must remain focused. If you can master this one thing, I believe this will eliminate a lot of unnecessary setbacks. Anytime you are trying to accomplish something big that is going to make an impact on thousands of lives there are going to be distractions to try to ambush, hinder, or block what God wants accomplished in the earth. It is not a matter of if they come but when they come.

Let's look at the meaning of the word distract.

Distract: to draw away or divert, as the mind or attention: to disturb or trouble greatly in mind; beset: disconnect, lead away, disturb, harass, puzzle, throw off, trouble, torment.

One of the things I want you to understand is distractions come in various forms and disguises. The devil knows that he cannot stop God's plan for your life but if he can get you to forfeit your own blessings through self-sabotage he will.

I cannot even begin to tell you how many major distractions I have allowed and dealt with throughout my life. In times past I never really recognized them as distractions because they were often disguised and hiding in relationships, haters, strife, confusion, rejection, torment, discouragement, attacks and the list goes on and on. The plot of the enemy is to keep you from recognizing distractions as a distraction. A sure way to tell if you're looking at a distraction is anything or anybody that comes to disturb or trouble the will of God for your life. Anything that diverts your attention from your divine purpose, and the plans of God being fulfilled, is a distraction.

So many times the devil will bring things, situations and people in your life to divert your attention away from the very things and people who will lead you to produce a prosperous life. If you noticed one of the definitions of the word distract means to disturb or trouble greatly in mind. One of the greatest distractions the enemy will use is people. I'm sure you can relate to this. Distractions can come through unhealthy relationships with people on the job, friends, people in the church, and even people in your family. The reason he will use people as a major distraction to try to hinder or block your destiny is because people can affect your soul and mind. People can tap your emotional realm and the devil knows that he can use people to rob your peace and joy. He knows he can use people to affect your health. He uses people to bring mental torment through the things they may do and say.

You must be careful of the people you allow into your life, mind, soul, and emotions who may be irrelevant to your destiny. The devil will often use people closest to you that can affect you and hit you right where it hurts. Beware of people that bring about confusion in your life because God is not the author of confusion; He is the God of peace.

Very often we want to be validated and accepted by those close to us, which sometimes leaves us vulnerable to the negative influences of people. I want to share a personal story with you about how I opened myself up to a major distraction through a dysfunctional toxic relationship.

The first time I got married I was very young. I had to be about 19 or 20 years old. It was so long ago it almost seems hard to believe that this was my life. At that age I did not know who I was and I did not have a sense of my purpose.

During that time my mother was going through her own drama trying to get herself together so she decides that she was putting everybody out the house. I felt pressured not having anywhere to go and moved in with my boyfriend at the time and shortly afterwards I ended up getting married. As I look back now I realize he was sent in my life from the pits of hell. Little did I know the enemy had a trap set for me because of the call of God that was upon my life. The enemy used him to try to literally destroy me. My life was constantly being threatened as I was being physically abused and to top it off I later found out that he was a drug dealer.

How crazy was that; one of the biggest distractions of my life. Now do you see how distractions come disguised? Sometimes we think, "Oh I was just in a bad relationship." No, that was a major distraction to throw you off course. It happens so you cannot walk in your divine purpose.

Have you ever felt like you have gone through one thing after the next? This is the history of my past. It seems as if I have repeatedly made one bad decision after another wondering will this vicious cycle ever end. Many times there are spiritual dimensions where satanic plots and schemes are incubated waiting for the most opportune time for their manifestation. The enemy will watch your patterns and launch a series of attacks to keep you living in a realm of distractions.

Some people are too easily distracted. This is what I want you to do. Identify the areas where you know you are easily distracted so you can break the pattern and stop allowing it to control your life. Once I identified the things that were easily distracting me, I finally found the key to breaking the vicious cycle of distractions. It was not until I became focused and developed discipline with a lifestyle of consistency that things started to change and shift in my life.

CHAPTER 6

Stay Focused Develop Discipline And Be Consistent

"Consistency Is The Key To Breakthrough."

The first rule of thumb in becoming focused is to admit that you need to be. You cannot change anything unless you are willing to admit there needs to be a change. You must be willing to say, "I have a problem and I need deliverance in this area of my life." For example, if you lack focus then admit that you need help focusing. Although I have never been diagnosed with ADD I remember all throughout high school I couldn't pay attention long enough to save my life. My ability to focus in school was a constant struggle for me, which carried over into my adult life. When I finally recognized this was an issue I was able to find strategies that helped me to strategically focus on purpose.

There is no shame in having struggles. The shame is in not dealing with them. So many times the devil will make people feel embarrassed and ashamed about their dysfunctions instead of embracing the spirit of truth so deliverance can take place.

Having a lack of focus will cause you to miss out on many opportunities, especially when you don't have the ability to focus long enough to establish discipline in your life. Most people don't have the discipline it takes to be consistent and it takes all the above to accomplish anything worth having in life.

Developing Discipline And Consistency

We talked a little bit about consistency at the end of chapter three but let us dig a little deeper. Let's look at the difference between consistency and discipline. With discipline, you must develop daily or regular habits that will produce your desired result. You need discipline when there is something that has to be established or developed. With discipline, there is often a regimen that develops or improves a skill, or there is training involved. You have to set and maintain a system of rules. Discipline requires self-control, restraint, preparation and practice, then it takes consistency to carry out or to maintain the discipline.

To be consistent means constantly adhering to the same principles; the same course or the same form. It means to be persistent, steady, or unchanging. For example, in prayer, I have developed the habit of self-control. I have developed a prayer regimen; a disciplined lifestyle of getting up, and praying every single day. It is a lifestyle that I had to develop. It did not happen overnight, but rather happened over the years. I had to be consistent in order to maintain the discipline.

So now, because I have developed a disciplined prayer life, I maintain that discipline by being consistent. I understand that prayer is the birthing place for all things and consistency is the key to breakthrough. You can apply this same principle to any and every thing.

If you don't master discipline and consistency you will never be able to build wealth or fulfill the will of God in your life. The road to prosperity is a process.

Loose Your Money – Make Money Obey You

Are You Willing To Pay The Price?

Not everybody is willing to pay the price to produce a lifestyle of wealth and success. There are a lot of ministers and leaders who desires the results of success but are not willing to do the necessary things it takes to manifest success. I use leaders as an example because they are who I am called to minister to. Most leaders want to wear the image of prosperity, but are too lazy and lack the discipline to pay the price. I have seen so many leaders so eager to speak into people's lives but yet won't take the time to develop discipline and consistency to birth an authentic prosperity anointing.

It vexes my spirit to see ministers who won't take the time to properly position themselves for wealth. The day for following unsuccessful leaders is over. Now days most preachers are more concerned with launching a ministry and being in authority status, rather than being concerned about being authentic.

I refuse to stand before people talking about money, prosperity or anything else and not be an example. God will not even allow me to minister or teach anything that I have not authentically birthed in my own life. I just cannot comprehend how a person can have a title, but yet have no mantle or results of success. Today's leaders do not want to pay the price to birth authentic prosperity oil, yet they want to be in somebody's face teaching. It's not that they don't have the potential or the gifts but it must be properly developed through discipline and consistency.

Being Disciplined And Consistent Is Necessary For Success

Many times people think discipline and consistency are not necessary to produce success. That is the wrong mindset to have. I challenge you to locate the areas where you need to get focused, develop discipline and be consistent. It may be in your work ethic. Maybe you are lazy. If so just say, "I am too lazy to be prosperous, that is why I am broke. I am too lazy to do what it takes and I am too lazy to do the work." You got to admit it, to defeat it. You cannot make excuses for your lack of success. Now day's people don't like to be challenged and deal with truth.

You may not even be disciplined enough to do what is necessary for prosperity to flow into your life but if you want your money to be loosed, you are going to have to be focused enough to develop discipline and apply consistency. Developing discipline and being consistent is not about a feeling, it is about doing what you know that will produce results. Sometimes you may have to do the same thing over and over until you see the manifestation, even when you don't feel like it. But always remember that consistency is the key to breakthrough.

Protect Your Investment

There is no way that I would be consistent for several months, or years, to develop discipline in a particular area of my life only to let it die. Think about this, it only takes 18-21 days to develop a habit, but where most people miss it is they don't know how to maintain the habit they develop with consistency. For example, if you can discipline yourself to go on a diet and lose weight, when the diet is over you must maintain your weight with consistency applying the necessary required things so you won't go back to the same old habits you had before the diet. This is the same principle you apply to anything, especially when acquiring money. Once you develop discipline in a thing, you must apply consistency to maintain it.

You must protect your investment with persistence and consistency. You cannot have a give up spirit, one minute you are with it and the next minute you are tired, and do not want to keep it going. I don't know about you but I have labored too hard and too long to quit, or give up something just because it seems hard or does not look like anything is happening. Another one of the devil's biggest distractions is to make you think what you are doing is not working. If he can get you to take your eyes off the prize, then that means your faith can't operate. The devil knows how to play mind games. Every time the devil comes with that deception I can hear my spiritual father's voice saying to me, "your faith will only take you to the point of your focus." And it takes focused faith to produce prosperity.

When a farmer sows seed into the ground, he understands the principle of seed, time and harvest…Therefore, he must protect his investment. How does the farmer protect his investment? He waters his seed daily. A farmer would never spend all his time in the field, breaking sweat plowing and tilling the ground, laboring in the hot sun, only to say "Well this stuff is not working. I don't see anything. I guess I won't water the field anymore." He is not going to do that, why because he worked too hard. He has too much seed in the ground right? He will protect his investment by consistently watering his seeds. It takes consistency to reap a harvest in life, especially money. A farmer will always prepare his field properly, in order to yield a harvest. You must think like a farmer by cultivating and protecting your field daily with consistency especially when you have seeds planted towards your prosperity.

Establishing discipline in your life enforcing it with consistency will give you authentic prosperity and absolutely nobody can take the credit but God.

CHAPTER 7

Let God Establish A Testimony In You

"You Must Commit To The Process."

Whenever God is trying to establish a testimony in your life, there is going to be adversity. I am sitting here with tears in my eyes as I am writing this chapter because one of the greatest challenges I have found when God is establishing a testimony is allowing patience to have her perfect work. The bible declares in James 1:4 to let patience have her perfect work that you may be perfect and entire wanting nothing. You cannot rush the process when a testimony is being developed in your life. You have to walk out the process while allowing endurance and steadfastness to do a thorough work. God wants the testimonial to be complete and in the process He wants you to be mature and perfected in order to produce a finished work. I don't believe that God will send you out premature or half done.

Think about when you are baking something in the oven, you don't want it to be half done; you want it to be complete. So many times we come out unfinished without completing the process. We want a microwave blessing. We don't want to commit to the process to experience the fullness of what God desires to accomplish in our lives. God wants you to be fully-developed, with no defects, lacking nothing.

When I reflect back on the things that I tried to make happen in my life, I am so glad that God blocked those things and did not allow me to step out prematurely because of my impatience. I thank God that His grace showed up and caused me to commit to the process and stay the course to walk it out. There were times I thought I was ready, only to realize that I wasn't.

Loose Your Money – Make Money Obey You

Do Not Fight The Process

People will sometimes do the wrong thing by trying to help God out when it appears as if He is taking too long to show up. This reminds me of how in the Bible, when God told Abraham and Sarah that He was going to bless them with a son. Instead of waiting on God they got impatient and as a result, Ishmael was born. I don't know about you but I have given birth to a lot of Ishmaels in my life by trying to do things my way instead of waiting on God.

We must learn how to trust God and do not fight the process. Go with the rhythm of God's divine flow, even when the process seems to take longer than you anticipated. When you resist the path that God has chosen for you, and decide to do things your own way, you will create an Ishmael and frustrate His grace in your life.

Commit to the process. It is not about you but it is about the thousands of lives you will touch through your testimony. It is about you helping others. Everything that I have ever gone through God has established an authentic testimony on the inside of me because I finally chose to commit to the process. I wouldn't have it any other way because when it is authentic, that is when it carries true power.

When you commit to something that means you are in it for the long haul, no matter what. No matter what the circumstances, no matter what comes your way. You want your testimony to be authentic when you are sharing how you overcame. What comes from the heart touches the heart, because it is real, and genuine.

Committing to the process requires you taking off the limits. At this point in my life I have completely taken off the limits in allowing God to have his way to do what He wants to do. When you take off the limits, you are saying, "Not my will, but your will Lord, have your way in every area of my life." Remove the limitations and be willing to die to yourself, to your will, to your emotions and accept God's way even when you don't understand the whys.

For most of my life, I could be asking God "Why?" But the why becomes irrelevant when you know the Who. There must be a strong level of trust in letting God establish the testimony that He wants to establish in your life but he needs your cooperation.

Going Through The Fire

Yes, there will be times when you will go through the valley of the shadow of death but the key is going "through." When you allow yourself to go through, you are going to come out on the other side like pure gold. In order for gold to be pure, it has to go through the purification process. It has to pass through the fire. There are seasons in life that you are going to go through fire. You are going to be tried to be purified, to remove all impurities in your life to make you fit to carry the oil of prosperity. Ask yourself; can you carry the prosperity oil? Can you carry the oil of the anointing? Can you carry wealth? Can God trust you even when things don't go the way you planned? Even when trials and storms come, will you be able to carry the oil? Will you be able to pass the test?

You may ask, "Why am I going through all of this stuff?" You cannot think it is strange when you are faced with abnormal adversity in your life, especially when there is greatness on the inside of you. All hell will break loose against you when you are carrying the wealth anointing and prosperity oil. You cannot be moved by what you see in the natural. Trials are designed to make you come up, not give up.

Loose Your Money – Make Money Obey You

The Fight Of My Life

1 Peter 4:12-13 (KJV) – "Beloved, think it not strange concerning the fiery trial which is to try you, as though some strange thing happened unto you: But rejoice, inasmuch as ye are partakers of Christ's sufferings; that, when his glory shall be revealed, ye may be glad also with exceeding joy."

Because of the assignment that is on my life to be a blessing carrier and help people all around the World loose money I have had many attacks, many storms, blizzards, hurricanes, tornadoes, and earthquakes in my life. I have experienced unusual and strange things through the years. You name it, I have been through it but I will not and cannot be moved. Even when I knew I was fighting for my life. I had two choices, either I commit to the process, and allow patience to have her perfect work, and allow God to establish an authentic testimony in my life or I quit. Those are our only options. Quitting, for me, is never an option. I have never been a quitter. I have labored too hard and too long.

I know what it is like to be broke. I remember many days robbing Peter to pay Paul with a negative balance in my checking account. I also remember having to file bankruptcy not knowing what else to do because I was so deep in debt. Before I remarried, I experienced being a single parent raising a child, therefore, I know what it is like to be a mother struggling and trying to make ends meet. I know what it feels like to have the repo man show up at your door step and the list goes on and on.

Have you ever felt like you are working hard and it seems like nothing you are doing is fruitful? I have been there too. There may be times where you are the only one who believes what God has called you to do, but you still have to walk the process out. I often compare the story of my life to Noah in the bible. I can only imagine that Noah's family laughed at him as he was building that ark, asking him questions like; "Why are you doing all that work? What are you doing all that for?" Every time Noah said it is going to rain, I am sure they talked about him behind his back and laughed. In the infant stages of what God was telling me to do to build wealth, I felt like Noah. It didn't look like anything was happening and I'm sure people wondered what I was doing and laughed at me. There will be times that people will laugh at you because you have stepped out in faith and taken the risk to take the limits off to obey God at all costs. But have a deaf ear to the talk and keep building that ark so God can get the glory. Never feel like you have to explain an unfinished work when God is still making it complete.

Building a business is similar to the groundwork of building a new home. The foundation has to be set before you can start to build. There is a lot of dirty work involved in the beginning stage. For example, the frame work must be put in place; all the plumbing and electrical wiring must go in before you can start to put in the pretty stuff; like laying the carpet, painting and etc. So it is with building wealth, there is a lot of labor that must take place on the front end. You have to have a solid, firm foundation when you are building wealth or it will not last. The infant stages are the hardest of building wealth because it is a process and it does not look like a testimony at first.

Many people are so ready to see the money without going through the process of laying the proper foundation of a business and all the labor that is necessary. I cannot tell you how many late nights and early mornings I have labored building my business. Sometimes I could not even tell the difference between day and night because I was just that hungry for things to change in my life. I was tired of producing the same result.

Loose Your Money – Make Money Obey You

I knew God was establishing a powerful life changing testimony in me during the process even when you could not see the results. I know I looked like a reproach. It seemed like the harder I worked the more broke I became. I even had family tell me, "Why are you doing all of that? You need to go get you a real job." But something on the inside of me would not quit because the desire to prosper was stronger than the voice of the enemy and I had a word from God.

I knew I was in the fight of my life for prosperity. I was doing all the right stuff; I was doing everything that God told me to do; and it still didn't look like anything was going to happen, just like Noah. It did not look like it was going to rain like God said. If I were a betting woman, I am willing to bet Noah said, "It doesn't look like it is going to rain, Lord. How long do I have to keep doing this? It has been years since I have been building this ark and I have not seen anything rain yet? I keep following your instructions, did I miss it somewhere Lord? Everybody keeps laughing at me. When in heck is it going to rain Lord?" Here I was building this business following God's divine instructions but could not see even a drop of prosperity.

I went through the mental torment and the mind battles like when the devil asked Eve in the garden, "Did God really tell you that?" The devil will use people to question what God told you to do. That is why you have to be careful who you share your dreams and visions with.

You must fight the good fight of faith. Timothy says we should hold on to our faith and good conscience, which some have put away and have become shipwrecked. You must stay the course so you can see the promise. Keep doing what you know is right, even when it doesn't seem like it.

Fight The Good Fight Of Faith

Hebrews 11:1, "Now faith is the substance of things hoped for, the evidence of things not seen."

Stand strong and firm on what you know. It is about a knowing. You have to know that God is there, even when He seems distant and silent. People look at my glory, but they don't know the story. You can never judge a man's prosperity because you don't know what that person did to get to the place where they are.

Many people look at me and they see the materials things or they see the blessing on my life, but what they don't know is even when I knew the blessing was on my life, I felt like I was cursed. I literally felt like I was walking under a dark cloud, but in my spirit I knew with everything on the inside of me that God called me to pour prosperity oil into the lives of thousands all around the world. At the time I had no idea I would be writing this book. This book was birthed from my tears of pain, to my prayer closet, through my personal worship and every financial principle I have applied. God had to establish an authentic testimony in me. It did not happen overnight. God will never fail you. His Word cannot lie. Every promise is yes and amen. I had to stand on the word of God, even when I looked like a reproach to people around me, when people were talking about me. Now I can say, "Look what the Lord has done."

You are going to be tested to see if you are solid and if your money can be built on a firm foundation so it will last. You are going to go through what I call the money test to see if God can trust you. You cannot bypass or escape the money test. The purpose is to see if you can hold the prosperity oil, to see if you have cracks in your vessel. Can you hold the oil of prosperity? God wants to clothe you in the blessing, but can you be trusted? Can God trust you with money? Let's see if you have passed the test.

1. The Tithe Test

Either you are a tither or you are not. There's no in between. You cannot be a tither sometimes when you feel like it or when it is convenient or when you think you have it. You will be tested with tithing. Sometimes it may take months to see if you are going to stick with it. Tithing consistently causes the windows of Heaven to be open to you, to pour out a blessing that there won't be room enough to receive it according to Malachi 3:10. I believe blessings come through ideas, insight, and concepts that will produce wealth. I have enough ideas, concepts, witty inventions and things to keep me busy for the next ten years. God has been pouring out an overflow. I have many things written down that is difficult to keep up with it all.

The tithe is your covenant connection to God. Can God trust you with the tithe? Will you be faithful? That is going to determine how much abundance will come into your life. It will determine if you will be able to wear the blessing and the garment of prosperity.

Ye are cursed with a curse: for ye have robbed me, even this whole nation. Bring ye all the tithes into the storehouse, that there may be meat in mine house, and prove me now herewith, saith the Lord of hosts, if I will not open you the windows of heaven, and pour you out a blessing, that there shall not be room enough to receive it.
And I will rebuke the devourer for your sakes, and he shall not destroy the fruits of your ground; neither shall your vine cast her fruit before the time in the field, saith the Lord of hosts. When you bring the tithe, God will rebuke the devourer. The devourer shall not destroy the fruit of your ground, neither shall your vine cast her fruit before the time in the field. That is your harvest, your wealth.

Kim K. Sanders

Aren't you tired of having holes in your pocket? I know I was. (Malachi 4:8-11)

I have been a tither for many years. It is not an option, but a privilege and an honor because it is God who gives me the power to get wealth. He gives me the ability and the endowment to get wealth. You must give God what belongs to him with reverential fear.

2. The Giving Test

Can God trust you to be a distributor for him? Can He use you for money to flow through? Whenever God chooses you to be a distributor of finances for him, and for his kingdom, He is trying to get something not only through you, but something to you. For example, let us say you are believing God for a new home and you have money saved. What would you do if God speaks to you and says, "I want you to give the money that you have saved for your down payment to Jane Doe, she is about to lose her home?" Can He trust you to obey?

I will never forget the day God challenged my husband and I with this particular test several years ago, I remember it like it was yesterday. God spoke to me one Saturday night and said, "I want you to pay off your car and give it away." God was very specific to who we were to give the car to. My immediately response was, "Okay Lord, but you are going to have to speak this to my husband." Well the very next day we were in the car coming home from Church and to my surprise my husband said, "You know what, the funniest thing happened to me during the praise and worship. God spoke to me and said for us to give away this car." God even spoke to him the person's name. I will never forget that as long as I live. We drove down the street rejoicing and immediately obeyed God's instruction. A few short years later God blessed me to drive my dream car.

Loose Your Money – Make Money Obey You

Will you pass the giving test? Will you give where he tells you to give? Money belongs to God. God created money therefore He understands the purpose of money. If you want to know the purpose of a thing you go to the original creator of it. God is the creator of money. God desires that you prosper. He delights in your prosperity. You cannot talk about money without talking about God. It all belongs to him.

> ***Psalm 24:1 – "The earth is the Lord's and the fullness thereof…"***

God created money, so he ought to know what you need to do with it.

3. The Obedience Test

I believe that obedience is key in passing the money test. A part of us giving our car away was to test our obedience as well as our giving. You must be willing to do whatever God tells you to do. It takes a significant amount of trust to obey God. Many times obedience requires sacrifice. Think about when Abraham was about to sacrifice his son Isaac on the alter. I'm not sure if I could have taken my only son to be a sacrificial offering. God always knows what is ahead of you. He knew that there was going to be a ram in the bush as Abraham obeyed. You have to pass the obedience test so God can trust you.

4. The Handling Of Money Test

Are you a compulsive spender, or are you selfish and hoard money? Are you utilizing money properly? God will allow you to have seasons or trinkets of money to see how you will handle it. He will allow you to see a little bit here and a little bit there to give you an opportunity to obey, before the abundance comes into your life to see if you are going to pass the test. God may give you an increase, but He may also ask you to give more. God will test you to see if He can trust you with more.

It is not enough to make a lot of money but it is about learning and knowing how money works. We must understand money is an instrument. Money is a vehicle in the earth and a tool God uses to put you in position to be a blessing. It is not about showing off with cars, houses and bling although there is nothing wrong with having nice things. True wealth is the ability to create progress to help elevate the community and the lives of the people around you. We must learn how to properly utilize money and reproduce it.

5. **The Faith Test**

When it does not look like anything is happening, will you still be faithful and trust God? God is not going to allow you to be tempted "above that which you are able" (I Corinthians 10:13). "There hath no temptation taken you for such as is common to man." In other words the enemy can only tempt you in the natural realm. The only thing that is common to man is the carnal realm where the enemy tempts and where he attacks. If he can get you to stay in the carnal realm, then that is where he can get you to lose faith and hope. The word of the Lord says, But God is faithful, who will not suffer you or allow you to be tempted above that which you are able.

I have red boxing gloves in my home that are symbolic of the blood, and spiritual warfare. It reminds me that I am a winner and I cannot be defeated. One thing I know is the enemy cannot come at me except in the carnal realm, which is why I have to live in the realm of the spirit where the enemy cannot trespass. If the devil can tempt you and get you to come out the realm of the spirit and get you into the natural, he will steal your focus.

You might as well go on and go through the process and stop fighting it and let God establish an authentic testimony in you, especially when it comes to money. You can't fake that. You can try to look good like you got it together, but eventually it's going to show up in your life.

God will never allow you to be tempted above that which you are able, but will with the temptation also make a way of escape that you are able to bear it. The way of escape is through the word of God and your spiritual weapons. The enemy will try to break you, as he attempted to break me but the enemy cannot break me. When he cannot break you, he will come through other ways. He will try to come through your friends, family, children, coworkers, church members or whoever will yield to him. Make a decision to stand strong and pass the faith test.

Be The Example Of Authentic Prosperity

The days of following unsuccessful leaders are over. I made a decision long time ago I refuse to stand before people talking about prosperity and have nothing in my life that represents God or wealth. I said to God, "Make me an example of who you really are. Make me an example of total life prosperity."

The prosperity in my life is authentic because it was built on a solid, concrete, firm foundation. When the storms of life come I will not be moved. I will stand firm because the fight in me will always be greater than any fight I will ever be in. The greater one lives on the inside of me.

Kim K. Sanders

1 John 4:4, "You, dear children, are from God and have overcome them, because the one who is in you is greater than the one who is in the world. (NIV)

It is never too late to prosper, when God gives you a plan and a strategy to walk out. He wants to develop that testimony in you and allow it to be pure and come to full maturity. I stand in a position pouring prosperity oil all around the world where I can make an impact and a difference in the lives of thousands and multitudes because I did not fight the process. I allowed patience to have her perfect work in my life.

CHAPTER 8

Pray It Through

"You Must Command Your Money To Be Loosed And Make It Obey You."

As you explore the pages in this chapter, I believe this is the most important chapter of this book you will read. We have gone through the practical principles to loose your money but here is where the rubber meets the road. Here is where we will separate the babies from the sons. You are going to learn the spiritual principles and the spiritual laws that will make money obey you only if you apply what I am about to teach you. .I can only tell you what I have done and what I know works. I cannot tell you anything outside of that because it would not be authentic. It would just be my opinion. This is more than just words on a page, there will be an impartation through this chapter that is going to affect your spirit, if you open up your heart to receive and let the Holy Spirit come in and have His way.

Many times people want to see the manifestation of money and don't because they either lack the practical principles while applying the spiritual laws or they put the practical principals to work but neglect the prayer closet and fail to apply spiritual laws. With me being in business and in ministry, it is kind of hard to separate the two, especially when I know that money comes from God, and understand that it takes the heavens to loose money. All you have read to this point works together. Success is based on a combination of both natural and spiritual principles. You must have both; you cannot escape spiritual laws and expect to prosper.

You may be asking what about people who have money that do not have a relationship with God? If you understand spiritual laws you will know that the rain falls on the just as well as the unjust.

That ye may be the children of your Father which is in heaven: for he maketh his sun to rise on the evil and on the good, and sendeth rain on the just and on the unjust.(Matthew 5:45).

Spiritual laws will work for whoever applies them because they work exactly like natural laws work; that is why is it important to have a consistent life of prayer in order to activate those spiritual laws. The bible declares in James 5:16 "...The effectual fervent prayer of a righteous man availeth much." I have found that most Christians do not have a balance when it comes to applying natural and spiritual laws; it is either to one extreme or the other.

A lot of people in the body of Christ claim to be such prayer warriors, but if a person is a powerful prayer warrior, then why are they broke? You mean to tell me such a person cannot even muster up enough prayer to birth prosperity? Obviously there is something missing. So let us take this journey to find the missing pieces to the prosperity puzzle, which will give you the treasures of darkness and hidden riches of secret places.

The Mind Of God Concerning Prayer

To understand the principles of prayer we have to understand the mind of God. God can do nothing in the earth unless He does it through man. It would be illegal because God has sworn Himself to His Word.

I have sworn by myself, the word is gone out of my mouth in righteousness, and shall not return, That unto me every knee shall bow, every tongue shall swear. (Isaiah 45;23)

We have to understand and respect God's established authority that has been set. Prayer was born out of God's plan for man's assignment on earth to rule, to have authority. Prayer was established when God said in Genesis Chapter 1:26 *"....let them have dominion."* These four words are critical in understanding the foundation of how prayer was established.

Loose Your Money – Make Money Obey You

The amplified bible says; *"...let them have complete authority"* and the NIV says *"...let them rule."* God gave man authority to rule and reign in the earth. When God declared "Let them rule" He gave up His legal right to rule in the earth and a law went into effect, now He can only interfere or have legal access to invade the earth realm except by and through man.

God will never violate His Word. Any law of God is a law to God. He is faithful to His Word. Psalms 119:89 says **"Forever, O Lord, thy word is settled in heaven."** This means God's word is already established.

Established means to found, institute, build, or bring into being on a firm or stable basis, to bring into existence; to install or settle in a position, place; to put beyond doubt or to prove; to form, organize, decree, make firm or stable, to institute (as a law) permanently by enactment or agreement.

God's Word is set in for the long haul; it has already been set up and set in order, it isn't going anywhere. It is here to stay, it's finished, it's planted, it's sure, it's valid, it cannot be reversed. The Word of God is unmovable, unchanging, it's unopposed which means it doesn't matter what you think about it, it's already so, it has already been decided, whether you believe it or not, whether you agree or not.....all you need to do is agree and comply.

We must understand that God magnified His Word above His Name. God places His Word above Himself, submitting Himself to the power of His own Word, so in other words when God speaks, He is obligated to obey His own Word because of His integrity.

"*...for thou hast magnified thy word above all thy name." (Psalms 138:2)*

We are to pattern after God being that we are made in His image and His likeness and speak His Word, just like He did. Everything that God created He did it by speaking it into existence. We will discuss this further in this chapter.

You see man is a spirit with a soul and physical body and only spirits with physical bodies can legally function in the earth realm. God made Himself subject to this law. God must have the agreement and cooperation of a person for whatever He desires to do in the earth, which is why prayer is so critical in the life of the believer because this is an established law.

Prayer is simply man giving God the legal right to interfere in earth's affairs, to have influence in the earth. Better yet, prayer is man exercising his legal authority on earth to invoke heaven's influence on the earth.

If we don't pray God cannot intervene in the earth. We the church have taken on a mentality of defeat before we even go into prayer, so we go into prayer with a defeated mind set and come out worse than the way we entered in. We must take responsibility for the earth by taking the responsibility in our prayer life.

Money Was Created To Obey You

Prayer is the birthing place for all things. This is the place where you make money obey your command. Whatever happens in the natural must first happen in the spiritual realm. You must pray for your money to be loosed from the heavens in order to see the manifestation of money in your life. Let us take a look at the scriptures that gives man the authority to determine what happens on earth.

Verily I say unto you, whatsoever ye shall bind on earth shall be bound in heaven: and whatsoever ye shall loose on earth shall be loosed in heaven. (Matthew 18:18)

As a Christian we must understand the power and authority that we really possess here in the earth. A powerful truth I have come to understand is; money was created to obey me, not for me to obey or be in bondage to it. Money was created to obey you just like any and everything else. It is no different than God giving man dominion in the earth.

Loose Your Money – Make Money Obey You

And God said, Let us make man in our image, after our likeness: and let them have dominion over the fish of the sea, and over the fowl of the air, and over the cattle, and over all the earth, and over every creeping thing that creepeth upon the earth. (Genesis 1:26)

We see in the scripture above that we are made in the image and likeness of God. So, therefore we have the ability to produce like God, because a seed produces after his own kind.

> *Genesis 1:24, "...and God said let the earth bring forth the living creature after his kind: cattle and creeping thing and beasts of the earth after his kind. And it was so."*

> *Genesis 1:26, "And God said let us make man in our image, after our likeness, and let them [meaning mankind] have dominion."*

God gave you dominion and authority to rule in the earth. God also blessed mankind and command him to be fruitful meaning to produce.

And God blessed them, and God said unto them, Be fruitful, and multiply, and replenish the earth, and subdue it: and have dominion over the fish of the sea, and over the fowl of the air, and over every living thing that moveth upon the earth.

How did God produce? He spoke to what he created. Keep in mind you are created in the image and in the likeness of God.

> *"...the earth was without form and void and darkness was upon the face of the deep and the spirit of God moved upon the face of the waters. 'and God said'..." (Genesis 1:2-3)*

Everything Begins With The Word Of God

The only way you are going to be effective in commanding money to obey you is to pray the Word of God only, not all this old stuff that you hear folks praying just to be seen or be heard. Sometimes we get the wrong understanding about prayer. If you are not speaking the Word, you are not praying. It is only the Word of God that is recognized in the heavens. There is a realm that exists where your voice will be recognized in the spirit realm. It is the place where angels will harken to the voice of the Word of God coming out of your mouth. It is a realm where demons obey your command. It is the atmosphere where the spirit realm recognizes the sound of authority in your voice and all of heaven cooperates in bringing the Word of God to pass in your life. This is the place my friend, where whatsoever you bind on earth shall be bound in heaven: and whatsoever ye shall loose on earth shall be loosed in heaven. Only speaking the Word of God with power can penetrate and move the heavens to this capacity.

Too many Christians are praying amiss and not seeing results. You have the ability to speak the Word of God, and see it come to pass in your life. Even though this can apply to any and every area of your life, we are talking about loosing your money. If you are going to walk in such a realm you must learn how to properly speak the Word of God and pray it through.

Everything starts with the Word. When you are birthing anything, you must start in the beginning.

In the beginning was the Word, and the Word was with God, and the Word was God.

2 The same was in the beginning with God.

3 All things were made by him; and without him was not anything made that was made. (John1:1-3)

Verse one says the Word was God. Here we see that God and the Word are one. You cannot separate the Word and God. In verse three, we see that all things were made by him. Without him was not anything made that was made. If we know that the Word was God and God and the Word are one in the same, then it would be safe to say that all things were made by *"The Word" and without the "Word" not anything was made that have come into being.* According to this scripture all things came into existence through the Word. You make all things with the Word of God.

If we look back all through Genesis the first chapter, God spoke what he wanted to see with His words. He said and He saw.

And God said, Let there be light: and there was light. And God saw the light, that it was good: and God divided the light from the darkness. (Genesis 1:3-4)

In verse six God says *"...Let there be a firmament in the midst of the waters and let it divide the waters from the water."* Again in verse nine God said, *"...Let the waters under the heaven be gathered together unto one place."* Do you see the pattern here? He saw what He wanted to create, He spoke it and then His words obeyed Him. He was speaking those things that were not in existence into divine manifestation. God's words were filled with power and His words obeyed Him as they came out of His mouth because the Word and God are one.

When most Christians speak the Word Today it is void of power. You know why, because many of us have not become one with the Word of God. When you become one with the Word you are becoming one with God, filling yourself with the power of God. Keep in mind if you are created in the image and likeness of your Father, you are able to do what He does. The example has been set before us. As God began to pour this revelation into me over the years, my prayer life began to shift to new realms and dimensions of authority.

Our words are not recognized in the spirit realm when the Word of God does not really live inside of us. I am not talking about you being saved, or the Holy Spirit living inside of you, I am talking about the Word of God actually being alive in you, and coming out of you with power. Many people are not willing to make the sacrifices it takes to do this. If you want the Word to have power when you speak it out of your mouth, it must live, abide and dwell inside your spirit to the degree that when you speak the Word it will shift atmospheres and changes things. This requires becoming one with the Word.

You cannot have an effective prayer life and produce anything if the Word is void of power when you speak it out of your mouth. That is why you see so many people unable to produce anything because what they speak is not alive and it is not coming from a place of authentic power. When you operate in authentic power, things will obey when you speak. Things will shift when you walk into a room and open your mouth. Demons will flee at the sound of your voice. The authority on the inside of you will be able to command them to leave the scene, I know this from experience. They will have to obey your voice because your voice is recognized in the realm of the spirit. So it is when loosing money. You have the authority say, *"Money be loosed"* and it obey your command.

When you are one with the Word and it lives in you, it is alive. It is not just scriptures on a page, it becomes life and it all starts in the place of prayer.

I want to share a few simple but yet profound principles I apply in my personal life that I have discovered to becoming one with the Father to make money obey me.

1. You Must Live A Life Of Obedience

If you cannot master this first step, you will never be able to have an effective prayer life and make money obey your command. If you cannot obey God how in the world do you think anything in the spiritual realm will obey you? Only the plan and will of God for your life is what will stand and be recognized in the heavens before God. You will not be able to defeat the enemy and come against his tactics, plans, plots overthrow his strategies or annihilate his hidden agenda if you are out of God's will.

Jeremiah 29:11 says *"For I know the thoughts that I think toward you, saith the LORD, thoughts of peace, and not of evil, to give you an expected end."*

Loose Your Money – Make Money Obey You

You must learn obedience, meaning God's way, not the way you think things ought to be done, but rather according to God's Word. Anything you do in life should always line up with the Word of God. It is critical to know His voice in order to be obedient. Obedience is the first key in becoming one with the Word of God and making money obey.

2. You Must Practice the Presence of God

Practicing the presence of God in prayer and in worship is a sure way to become one with Him. When you become a yielded vessel and spend time in prayer you connect with God. When you spend time in worship you develop a love relationship with God and bring Him on the scene into your affairs.

In order for me to operate in the graces, gifts, and anointing that is on my life, God requires me to pray and worship a certain amount of hours daily. I am not saying that is something you have to do, but it is a part of my personal consecration. I would never preach my personal convictions or my personal consecration to anybody telling them this is what you need to do but there are certain things that I must do to maintain the anointing and oneness with God in my life.

Prayer is the birthing place for everything. I produce everything I do from a place of prayer. This book has been birthed from a place of prayer and worship. I spend a few hours in prayer every day, and then after I come out of prayer, I go into an enormous time of worship. Did you know that worship will loose your money? It is kind of hard to explain it in the natural but it is true. Worship can open doors. Your money can be loosed singing and worshiping, because God inhabits the praises of his people. Your worship brings God on the scene of your situation. He will come in your midst. Worship breaks the powers of the enemy. When you begin to worship, things are taking place that you know not of. It opens doors to the supernatural. When Paul and Silas were in prison they began to worship and pray and it opened the prison doors.

When Paul and Silas were in prison; they began to worship, and pray. It opened the prison doors. And at midnight Paul and Silas prayed, and sang praises unto God: and the prisoners heard them. And suddenly there was a great earthquake, so that the foundations of the prison were shaken: and immediately all the doors were opened, and every one's bands were loosed. (Acts 16:25-26)

If you need your prison doors of debt to be loosed then I suggest you begin to open up your mouth and get to singing and praying. My Spiritual Father always says, *"When you have the Word of God on your situation, you have God on your situation, therefore, your situation must change."* That is powerful. Sometimes I think we just take our affirmations and confessions lightly. We don't take the Word literally to be exactly what it says and to mean what it says.

Let your days be orchestrated by the Holy Spirit and learn to practice God's presence unhindered. Some things cannot be taught, they have to be caught. I decree and declare as you yield yourself in God's presence, God is going to break your invisible prison doors of debt through worship, and loose your money in the name of Jesus.

3. Meditate On The Word Of God

If you want your words to be like a force when you speak, everything you say must be in divine alignment with the Word of God. In order for the Word to live in you, you must meditate on it.

This book of the law shall not depart out of thy mouth; but thou shalt meditate therein day and night, that thou mayest observe to do according to all that is written therein: for then thou shalt make thy way prosperous, and then thou shalt have good success. (Joshua 1:8)

Meditating on the Word of God will allow you to make your way prosperous and cause good success to come into your life. One of the meanings of the word meditate in this scripture means to *mutter*. It also means to ponder, or to imagine. When you think on the Word of God you are turning it over and over in your head. You are going to have to turn the scriptures over and over in your mind muttering and confessing it out of your mouth continuously until it becomes a regular part of your pattern of thinking and your vocabulary. Once you get the Word in your heart, as a result of meditating it day and night, it will then become a creative force to speak out of your mouth full of power. When you confess the Word of God, it puts an image inside you. Nobody can say the Word like you say it. Your voice should be the greatest authority besides the voice of God.

You must keep the Word before your eyes and your ears so it can enter into your heart.

The Bible says in Proverbs 23:7, *"...For as a he thinketh in his heart, so is he...."* whatever you meditate on the most is what you are going to become. Your thoughts become a part of who you are.

Whatever you put before your eyes and ears it is going to get into your heart. What is in your heart will eventually come out of your mouth and out of the abundance of the heart, the mouth will speak.

A good man out of the good treasure of his heart bringeth forth that which is good; and an evil man out of the evil treasure of his heart bringeth forth that which is evil: for of the abundance of the heart his mouth speaketh. (Luke 6:45)

To speak words, is to produce. This is why it is important to meditate on the Word. If you want your money to be loosed, then you have to get the Word in your heart and the way you get it in your heart is through meditation.

4. Get Clothed In The Word And Pray It Through

It is not enough to just read the Word of God; you must be clothed in the Word at all times if you are going to be one with God and produce results in prayer. It has to be a part of you. Jesus spent an enormous time in prayer with the Father. Jesus modeled a lifestyle of prayer. When he was in the Garden of Gethsemane, he was getting ready to face his most crucial moment, and that is when he prayed with great intensity. He prayed it through until the end.

If you are going to birth anything in your life, there will be times of strong travail when you will have to pray with great intensity. When Jesus was in the garden praying, he said *"My soul is exceedingly sorrowful even unto death."* according to Mark 14:34.

There will be times when you don't know what to pray, this is when you pray in the Holy Ghost. When you pray in the Holy Ghost, you are praying the plans and will of God. You are bypassing your intellect and God is coming through you. You are a vessel for Him to birth forth things in the earth through prayer. God has to have a vessel to flow through in order for things to manifest in the earth. He will tell you what to pray. That is why the enemy will fight you on prayer. When you are praying in the Holy Ghost, you are also covering your ignorance. That is why I believe the devil fights people with the baptism of the Holy Spirit, with the evidence of speaking in other tongues. He doesn't want people to tap into that because he knows the power attached. The Holy Spirit will help you pray when you don't know what you should be praying because the Bible declares that the Spirit makes intercessions for us with groanings which cannot be uttered, or which cannot be articulated in your native language. You are praying the perfect prayer when you pray in the Holy Ghost.

When you get up in the mornings, start to decree and declare that your money is loosed, especially if God wakes you up during the fourth watch between the hours of 3am and 6am when miracles begin to take place. Declare the plans of God over your life. When you begin to make your affirmations, you are confirming all the things that you have prayed. That is how you loose your money. You have to loose it from the heavens. Say this out loud, "Money I command you to be loosed."

Command your money to be loosed from the heavens. In the amplified bible, it says ***"Truly I tell you whatever you forbid and declare to be improper and unlawful on earth must be what is already forbidden in heaven; and whatever you permit and declare***

Loose Your Money – Make Money Obey You

proper and lawful on earth, must be what is already permitted in heaven." (Matthew 18:18)

I believe it is improper and unlawful for you as a believer to be broke and live in poverty. Remember you make your way prosperous and cause good success to come to your house therefore you get to prophesy your future. God has given you the power to get wealth. You get to open your mouth and declare what is yours. Open up your mouth and speak the Word of God over your money and loose it. Command your money to obey you. Put yourself in a position where the spirit realm recognizes your voice, where angels will hearken to the voice of your words.

Romans 1:16, "For I am not ashamed of the gospel of Christ [that's the Word of God] for it [the Word of God] is the power of God unto salvation to everyone that believe…"

The Word of God is the power of God that will produce salvation. That word 'salvation' in the Greek means *soteria,* which means deliverance from the curse of the law. It also means health, preservation, safety, deliverance, prosperity, and victory. The Word of God is the power of God that will produce deliverance, prosperity, health, and victory. Now how powerful is that? I hope you caught that revelation.

The Word must be established in your heart first before it can be established or manifested in your life. That is why the devil fights to keep you away from the Word, because he knows the power of the Word if you come into agreement with it and engrave it in your heart and put it in your mouth. It will produce because of the covenant between God, Abraham and man through the Lord Jesus Christ.

Summons Your Money

Jesus is a powerful example to follow when it comes to speaking the Word with the authority to make it obey. Jesus spoke the Word and made the winds obey Him.

And they came to him, and awoke him, saying, Master, master, we perish. Then he arose, and rebuked the wind and the raging of the water: and they ceased, and there was a calm And he said unto them, Where is your faith? And they being afraid wondered, saying one to another, What manner of man is this! for he commandeth even the winds and water, and they obey him. . (Luke 8:24-25)

Another example is when Jesus summoned Peter to walk on the water. To summons means to call forth, to call to a place, call in or call into action, request.

And Peter answered him and said, Lord, if it be thou, bid me come unto thee on the water. And he said, Come. And when Peter was come down out of the ship, he walked on the water, to go to Jesus. (Matthew 14: 28:29)

Just like Jesus called Peter to come, we must summon our money to obey the same way.

Jesus also dealt with the devil and cast out demons on various occasions with the Word and they obeyed His command. God has given us authority over demons to obey our command, how much more can we use our words to make money obey?

I remember several years ago when I had a puppy. I had a beautiful black chow named Onyx. We spent a few weeks training in a dog obedience school. I was trained to make him obey the command of my voice. Eventually he was trained to obey my voice every time I gave him a command to do something, but it took repetition. This is exactly the same way you must train your money to obey your voice. If a dog can be trained to obey a human, how much more can money obey your command?

Begin to decree and declare the Word of God over your money. To decree means to command, ordain, or decide by decree; a formal and authoritative order; one of the eternal purposes of God, by which events are foreordained; an edict, law, etc, made by someone in authority.

Loose Your Money – Make Money Obey You

To declare means confession or acknowledgment; to announce, act of recognizing authority or truth of something; assertion of belief or knowledge. Bring forward, confirm, repeat, profess, reaffirm, publish, contend, to make known clearly or officially, to make a proclamation, to manifest or reveal.

Open up your mouth right now and make this confession:

"I decree and declare that my money is being loosed right now from the heavens. I command my money to be loosed in the earth daily; therefore, the heavens must loose my money daily.

Everywhere I go, the manifestation of money shows up in my life because I attract money everywhere I go. I never chase money. I attract money. Money hunts me down. It looks for me. Money knows how to find me. It finds me daily. Goodness and mercy follow after me all the days of my life. Money follows and chases after me everywhere I go. Every day there is a divine manifestation of money in my bank accounts. Begin to declare, "Money, I call you right now and I command you to manifest yourself." I sow, so I must reap. Men give back to my life daily, good measure, pressed down, shaken together and running over. The windows of heaven are wide open to me to pour out a blessing that there shall not be room enough to receive, causing an overflow of the blessing in my life. Money overflows in my personal life, my business, my bank account, and to my ministry. Money is flowing to me like a river right now, it never stops flowing. I have the ability and the power to produce as much money as I desire. The source of money lives in me.

Ideas, insight, concepts from the heavens come to me daily to produce millions of dollars. It is in my DNA. It abides in me. It dwells in me. It produces out of me. I produce millions of dollars daily because I am a money maker. When people come in contact with me, they come in contact with money."

You will find these confessions in the back of my book. This is what I confess daily as I spend time with God in prayer. This is the way you loose your money. Begin to give voice to the Word; and when you are consistent, and when you are diligent, money will obey your command. Angels will hearken to the voice of your words. Pray it through in confidence until you see the divine manifestation of your words in your life.

CHAPTER 9

You Can't Stop Me Devil!

"You Must Push Through The Resistance."

No matter what type of adversity you may go through in life there will be resistance and the temptation to give up. You must make a conscious decision that the fight in you must be greater than the fight you are in. I have had countless times where I had to decide, I refused to be defeated and I will not quit.

The first thing you must realize when you are in a spiritual battle is your battle is not against flesh and blood.

Ephesians 6:12-13, "For we wrestle not against flesh and blood, but against principalities against powers, against the rulers of the darkness of this world, against spiritual wickedness in high places…against spiritual wickedness in high places, wherefore take unto you the whole armor of God that you may be able to withstand in the evil day and having done all to stand."

Although you are fighting disembodied spirits, know that the battle is not your, it is the Lord's. Have the assurance knowing the greater one lives on the inside of you. Your greatest weapon to use in a spiritual battle is The Word of God. When you have the Word of God on your situation, you have God Himself on the situation therefore your situation must change. Now how assuring is that?

One of the greatest strategies of the enemy in a spiritual battle is to get you to cave in and quit before you see the manifestation of your breakthrough. For so many years the enemy has tried to stop me from tapping into loosing my money. Oh, but it is too late now and he cannot stop me. You must have the mentality of a warrior, quitting is not an option. You must stand and be clothed in the authority of the Lord Jesus Christ. You cannot loose money without bringing God on the scene, because we have an adversary, the devil, to content with that creates a lot of opposition and resistance. It is imperative to learn how to become a sniper in the realm of the spirit by targeting your prayers like arrows annihilating every hidden agenda of the enemy. I personally pray with a mission to hit bull's eye in the realm of the Spirit every time. I hit every fiery dart, tactic and scheme of the enemy with the Word of God, the blood and Name of Jesus by the power of the Most High God. You must shine the light of God's Word on every dark place the enemy hides and uncover his strategies, covert operations, and render them null and void.

Stop and decree this over your life right now, say this out loud: *"I arrest all interferences, every demonic influence and I dismantle all plans, plots and ploys against me, my household and my finances. I decree and declare that there will be no more negotiations, spiritual abortions or miscarriages and I overthrow all setbacks, sabotages, and disappointments. I obliterate satanic wombs, satanic incubations and every diabolical assignment designed to hinder, distract, frustrate, paralyze, block, delay, suppress or prevent the grace and will of God for my life. I prohibit and disallow satanic databases, satanic manifestations or satanic harassments and I forcefully resist all deceptions, lies and confusion from the powers of darkness. I pull down every stronghold, I come against every principality and I break every power of the enemy against me, my family and those connected and assigned to me. I decree and declare that we've been delivered from the powers of darkness and translated into the Kingdom of Jesus Christ, in Jesus name, it is so."*

This is the attitude that you must embrace if you are going to loose your money and make it obey you. You must push through the resistance to break through every opposing thing that comes your way.

Several Pastors in the Body of Christ teach their congregation, that our battle is not against flesh and blood, but against principalities against powers, against the rulers of the darkness of this world, against spiritual wickedness in high place, but I often wonder do we have a real revelation and understanding of what this really means. I can literally say that this scripture has become a reality in my life. All my life I have had to fight disembodied spirits. I have had countless ruthless attacks from the pit of hell in my life. I have had major attacks on my physical body. I have had mental and emotional attacks as well but I always win and come out with the victory.

Because of the anointing that rests on my life I definitely understand why the battle has been as intense as it has been in the past and even now. I finally know how to properly fight the powers of darkness. I know how to break through the struggle, the opposition and the warfare. I feel like I should have a PhD in deliverance.

Unexpected and unexplainable things will happen when you are fighting a spiritual battle. The good news is the devil knows he cannot stop the plan of God in your life. That is why he will bring all type of distractions, setbacks, roadblocks, and all types of things to get you to quit and forfeit God's will for your life. He knows that if you quit, you do not win. You cannot allow the enemy to have any ground.

The enemy will often use people to launch an attack against you. Sometimes it is those who are closest to you. The enemy will bring out the heavy hitters and use people who he knows will affect you the most. Then you have the naysayers, those are people who habitually express negativity. They are pessimistic, what I call joy killers, people who like to rain on your parade. Then you will always have instigators and haters. Let them do what they do because eventually they will ensnare a trap for themselves. Do not even waste your time or give your energy to people of that nature. Realize there are spirits working behind the things that you cannot see operating to cause these things in your life, especially when you know that you are doing all the right things.

Any time you are in a battle, you must have an undefeated mentality. You are in a battle whether you want to be or not, so you might as well learn the rules of engagement. It is imperative to be clothed in the whole armor of God to be able to stand against the wiles and tricks of the devil. In times of spiritual warfare, you must use spiritual weapons only to defeat the powers of darkness.

For though we walk in the flesh, we do not war after the flesh. For the weapons of our warfare are not carnal, but mighty through God to the pulling down of strongholds (2 Corinthians 10:3-4).

Let us discuss how you press through the struggle, opposition, the pain and the misery that comes along with spiritual warfare. How do you push through the resistance?

Keep Moving

Keep it moving and know that you are almost at the finish line. Anytime the attacks come with great intensify, that means you are at the verge of your breakthrough. You are right at the door. It is about to happen. You are making headway in the spirit; and the enemy's job is to get you to stop but you must stay focused and keep pushing. To push means to press forward, to continue, to proceed, to make one's way with effort or persistence against difficulty or opposition. In other words keep it moving. Push through. If you think about it, when you are in the gym and you are lifting weights; or you are climbing on that treadmill and you up the resistance, it becomes harder, so you have to press. You can feel the resistance when it comes. Resistance does not feel good, especially to the flesh but it is not about a feeling, it is about doing the right things that will produce results.

Loose Your Money – Make Money Obey You

My brother is a certified personal trainer and we used to work out together. He used to train me. We would have a designated time that we were going to meet at the gym and there were several times when I would seriously consider calling or texting and telling him, "Oh I can't make it today." You know how it is when you try to make up an excuse in your mind, why you can't do something. But something in me just could not say I am not coming because I knew that he was taking time out of his schedule, driving across town, just to help me. The least I could do was show up right? Even though there were many times I felt like not showing up and quitting, however, I am so glad I pressed through the mental resistance. But then somewhere along the process my mind stared to shift. After weeks and weeks of working out, I started to see results. When you have the persistence to press through and not quit you will see your desired results. I saw results because I did not quit.

Use Your Spiritual Weapons

God has given all of us weapons to use. You cannot fight this spiritual battle with the things of the natural. It is just not going to happen. Anybody who has ever accomplished any level of success has had opposition and resistance.

There are five weapons that I have personally used in battle to loose my money, some of which we have already covered in the last chapter, but I will address it from a different view point. These are major weapons, and each weapon is a powerful force within itself. This is not something you just do, and then quit. You must be discerning of which weapons to use in each season of your life. There are different phases and realms of prosperity. You should always continue increasing and upgrading in the financial realm. If you apply these principles, you will break through to the next realm. You may not master the use of all these weapons overnight, but you will know the weapons you have at your disposal.

Weapon # 1 – Prayer

Prayer is one of the most lethal weapons that you will use in spiritual warfare. We know that prayer is the birthing place for all things, but it is also a powerful weapon against the forces of darkness.

> *James 5:16, "...The prayer of a righteous person is powerful and effective. (NIV)*

It is not enough to just have a prayer life, but you must have a disciplined prayer life. The enemy will bombard your life with so many distractions that you don't spend time in the Word or in prayer. One must maintain a consistent prayer life in order to maintain the blessings of God. The average Christian will watch hours of television, and only spend five to ten minutes in prayer and wonder why they are broke. I am not saying to get rid of your favorite television shows but I am asking you to think about this; how can prosperity come to your house if you spend more time developing a life of entertainment more than spending time establishing your financial future in prayer?

> *2 Chronicles 7:14, "If my people, who are called by my name, will humble themselves and pray and seek my face and turn from their wicked ways, then I will hear from heaven, and I will forgive their sin and will heal their land.*

Prayer is a weapon, a force that you need in your life. Prayer is the place where I have learned how to break the powers of the devil. There have been times where my flesh does not feel like praying, but I have disciplined my flesh to become subject to my spirit and now I

Loose Your Money – Make Money Obey You

am in love with prayer. Do not compare your prayer life to anyone else's because there are different realms and dimensions of prayer. If the enemy can make you feel intimidated by someone else's prayer life then it will make you want to stop. His job is to make you think that what you are doing is not working, or to try to make you feel like God is not receiving your prayers, but start where you are and know that God hears you when you pray. The devil and all hell ought to know what time you get up to pray.

Weapon # 2 – Speaking The Word Of God

Death and life are in the power of the tongue: and they that love it shall eat the fruit thereof. (Provers 18:21)

You have the power and creative force in your mouth to speak life over your finances and command money to come forth. Of course the Word of God is the foundation for every weapon that you could possibly use because everything is established from the Word. Remember I told you that the Word of God is the power of God or force that will produce deliverance or that will produce your prosperity. It is the power of the Word that unlocks prosperity. Always know when you apply the force of God's Word in any situation, it will not come back empty.

So shall my word be that goeth forth out of my mouth: it shall not return unto me void, but it shall accomplish that which I please, and it shall prosper in the thing whereto I sent it. (Isaiah 55:11)

Weapon # 3 - Worship

Worship is a very powerful force against the powers of darkness. As I said in the last chapter, worship brings God on the scene because Psalms 22:3 says He inhabits the praises of His people.

Worship will take you behind the veil to experience the supernatural. Keep in mind that these are supernatural spiritual weapons that are mighty through God, which He has given us to be used in warfare that you cannot always explain; just like you cannot always explain spiritual attacks from the devil. As you begin to worship you can put a demand on your harvest to manifest in the earth. You can command money to come and obey through your worship. What makes worship so powerful is the power within; it is the man behind the worship that is filled with the power of God. As you increase in your intimate time with God in prayer, and as you have more of a desire for Him and His Word, it will begin to create a deeper level of worship on the inside of you.

The greatest level of worship is obedience. It is more than just singing a song, it has to be a lifestyle. Worship is about living a life of obedience. You cannot go behind the veil living a disobedient life. It is about totally surrendering your life completely to God; your mind, your will, and emotions. That is true worship. When you begin to get into that realm of I surrender all, it will create a deeper place of worship from your spirit.

Weapon # 4 – Giving

A lot of people don't think of giving as a weapon, but it is a very powerful weapon that will produce a powerful harvest if applied in good fertile ground. The devil fights people in The Body of Christ on giving. The Body of Christ has a hard time receiving the giving message especially in tithes and offerings. Most times those in the world will give to charity, and to things more so than some of us church folk, because they have the revelation and the understanding about the power that is attached to a seed.

Loose Your Money – Make Money Obey You

We must realize once a seed is planted it never leaves your life but yet God causes it to multiply and come back into your life and produce more than what you gave. When I look out my window, and see the peach tree in my backyard, every year I see so many peaches that comes from one seed. One seed that was planted that brought forth multiple peaches. To take it even a step further, just think of all the seeds that are in each of these peaches. This is exactly the type of harvest that we can expect when we sow our seeds.

Give, and it shall be given unto you; good measure, pressed down, and shaken together, and running over, shall men give into your bosom. For with the same measure that ye mete withal it shall be measured to you again. (Luke 6:38)

Weapon # 4 – Love

Like I said earlier, in this spiritual battle, the enemy will use people against us to get us to forfeit our own blessing but you must use the power of love as one of your weapons. God knows I have had to do this time and time again, even when it hurts the most. You may ask, what in the world does this have to do with loosing money? It has everything to do with you living in abundance because Galatians 5:6 tells us that faith works by love and it takes faith to reap. Love is a very powerful, weapon because the enemy will work overtime trying to get you into bitterness, strife and unforgiveness to get you to sabotage your blessing. I know it can be quite challenging to love some people but you must walk in love if you are going to live a prosperous life.

Always remember this: what God wants to do through you my friend, is greater than "anything" anybody has ever done to you. Don't allow anybody to hold you in a place of bondage by holding a grudge or by being a slave to the sin of unforgiveness. Who carries that type of power in your life? Make this confession out loud:

"I refuse to allow anybody to dictate and determine how I choose to feel about them. I will always be in control of my thoughts, emotions, feelings and actions. I will not give that power to anyone because I am in control.

I decree and declare that I will not be a victim to the sin of bitterness and unforgiveness. In the name of Jesus I loose all bitterness and unforgiveness in my heart right now towards _____ (call out each person's name). Now Lord I ask that you forgive me.

Father, I ask that you cleanse and heal my soul that I may glorify you in all that I do, in the name of Jesus. I say that love flows through me like a river, washing away all hurt, all disappointments and offenses. I choose to love at all times. I declare that love is deeply planted within me. My seeds are love, joy, peace, brokenness, compassion, and strength. I water my seeds daily. My seeds grow daily and produce life. I wear love and compassion as my garments. I'm clothed in God's love. God is love therefore I am love because I'm made in His image and in His likeness. I wear love daily, it is in my DNA, it is who I am. I am love because God is in me. When I look in the mirror I see love. When people look at me they see love all over me because it permeates from the inside out. I eat love, I drink love, and I breathe love. Love runs through my veins like a blood transfusion. The blood of Jesus cleanses and washes me. I receive my blood transfusion right now, in the name of Jesus amen."

Weapon # 5 – Fasting

If you are going to fulfill the will of God in your life I suggest you tap into the supernatural power of fasting. Fasting puts your spirit in a place of sensitivity where you can hear clearly. I have been living a lifestyle of prayer and fasting for over twenty five years. That is a long time. I remember years of fasting just because I wanted to become keen to God's voice and receive divine revelation from His Word. If you want to learn more about fasting, *"Fasting for Breakthrough"* by Lenika Scott is a very powerful book for you to read.

Fasting is a weapon that I have personally used to be able to tap into the supernatural. Fasting allows you to hear keenly into the realm of the spirit. You become more sensitive to God's voice and to the things of God and breakthrough comes as a result.

Fasting is not just about not eating food, it is about denying yourself, crucifying the flesh and bringing your flesh into subjection to your spirit so that your spirit man can rise up and be the dominant one. When you fast, you must submit yourself and subject yourself to the Word in prayer; otherwise it is not a fast but a diet. Fasting is emptying yourself, to be filled with the things of God.

Do Not Give Up

During your time of spiritual warfare, God will always send someone to encourage you. He will always send words of encouragement. He will send prophecies, prophetic utterances, prophetic words, the word of wisdom or the word of knowledge. He will send people along the way to let you know that he has not forgotten about you. The devil will try to wear you out, but do not give up. You must fight the good fight of faith. If it had not been for God using my spiritual father Prophet Leonard Ford throughout the years to speak into my life, I don't know what I would have done. Learn to appreciate the people that God sends in your life to be an encouragement to you.

I want to leave you with one of my personal quotes to chew on: *"How can you be too weak to breakthrough but yet too strong to keep bearing the pain?"*

CHAPTER 10

The Divine Manifestation

"You Must Attract Money, Never Chase Money."

When the blessing of God and the oil of prosperity is poured upon your life it will cause a divine manifestation of extravagant favor, and subsequently causing an overflow of abundance. When I tapped into this revelation, it shifted my mindset. I will never forget when God told me to stop chasing money and to start attracting money. This is when the game changed for me.

When you have an authentic anointing of wealth and prosperity upon your life, you will not chase money, you will attract money. Please do not get it twisted; I am not talking about putting in the necessary hard work to build wealth and pursuing your destiny or your business, but I am talking about literally chasing after money.

I hear a lot of people confess, *"I am a money magnet. Money is coming to me."* But their actions show different. I believe at some point we have all been guilty of chasing money. Some folks are just right out sanctified hustlers and I am not criticizing a person's hustle. It has never really been in me to be a hustler no matter how hard I have tried to be. But I have discovered there is an anointing to prosper and reap. I have finally discovered God never designed for me to follow after money. Goodness and mercy should follow after me. Money should follow you. You should attract money. Some people would disagree with that, but we are talking about the "divine" manifestation of money.

If you really think about it, it looks very unattractive to chase money. The word chase means to pursue in order to seize, overtake, to pursue with the intent to capture. It means to follow or devote one's attention to with the hope of attracting. I want money to be in pursuit of me. If you are chasing money it means you are the pursuer, not money. So many people are desperately chasing after money instead of learning how to position themselves to attract money.

Always remember, God has given you authority over money and you can make money obey you. This is something you have to practice. How do you get money to obey you? Use your authority. Money is supposed to obey you. If you don't get that in your mind and get that in your heart, it never will.

When The Windows Of Heaven Are Opened

When the windows of heaven are wide opened over you, God will bless you. This is where the blessing comes on your life. God will open the windows of heaven and pour out a blessing over you that there will not be room enough to receive.

Bring ye all the tithes into the storehouse, that there may be meat in mine house, and prove me now herewith, saith the Lord of hosts, if I will not open you the windows of heaven, and pour you out a blessing, that there shall not be room enough to receive it. (Malachi 3:10)

I believe that when the windows of heaven are opened and God pours out the blessing, it will come forth in the form of ideas, insights, and concepts from the Holy Spirit that will produce multiple streams of income. God will give you so many ideas and so many ways to make money that you won't be able to hold it all. I personally have enough things to keep me busy for the next 5-10 years.

Loose Your Money – Make Money Obey You

Uncommon Extravagant Favor Will Show Up

Here is where preparation meets opportunity. God will place opportunities before you when you are properly prepared. Everything in your life is now divinely aligned with God's will. When you have positioned yourself for prosperity to flow into your life doors of opportunity will open to you and extravagant favor will come on the scene. God will raise somebody up to raise you up.

You are ready for the divine manifestation to take place because you have done all of the necessary things required. You have done the practical and spiritual things. Now, God will raise somebody up to favor and feature you for the divine manifestation of what you have been waiting for because the windows of heaven are open above you. Applying uncommon principles will release uncommon favor.

Living In The Overflow

When the heavens are opened wide, it will bring about a steady unending flow of increase and prosperity in your life. This is called living in the overflow of life. Money will start to hunt you down. This is where the anointing will cause money and people to be attracted to you. This is where you move over into whatever your hands touch, it shall prosper. People will bless you everywhere you go because you wear the blessing like a permanent garment that cannot be removed. The blessing attracts prosperity and wealth. When something attracts, it gravitates to you like a magnet. You will gain the interest of people and the divine manifestation of being a money magnet will gravitate toward you. It's like a force that is causing money to be pulled to you. It is the anointing that will cause people to start to bless you effortlessly. You don't have to manipulate or beg people for money.

It just grieves my spirit to see people beg for money. Begging for money is chasing money, whether it's begging for a sale or begging for an offering, it's all the same. Let me explain. There is a difference between marketing, letting people know what you have to offer and harassing someone to buy your products. True marketing, is not telling people "you need to buy my products." True marketing is allowing them to see the value and benefits in what you're offering. For example, I offer all natural health and weight loss products to help others obtain divine health. I never flood social media with pictures of my products harassing people to buy my stuff. I simply invited them into my intriguing lifestyle creating irresistible marketing causing people to be captivated by my amazing weight loss. As a result people see the benefits of my products because I am the example and they spend hundreds of dollars with me. That is the ability to attract and not chase money.

With today's social media we see that people love to follow successful people. Once people see your success and the benefits of what you are offering then they will exchange money with you. That is how you attract money. People will see the anointing in your life and the anointing will attract money, you don't have to beg nobody to buy nothing from you.

To all ministers who are in a five-fold ministry, you don't have to stand on the pulpit and beg for an offering. There is an anointing to receive offerings. If The Body of Christ really understood how the kingdom of God is supposed to operate concerning tithes and offerings, then people would give the way they are supposed to and just maybe men and women of God would not feel intimidated as if they have to manipulate and beg people for money. As a minister of the gospel, always remember you are there to meet the needs of the people on behalf of the Father. When you meet the needs of the people in exchange and in return, the anointing on your life will demand people to give without you asking. I know that may be hard for some of you to believe and you may even disagree but I am a living witness. People sow and give into my life on a regular basis without me asking and when I stand before people to receive an offering in services my focus is not money. Most people give effortlessly because their need has been met. I am not saying that anything is wrong with taking up an offering; please do not misunderstand what I am saying. Of course, we must receive an offering to give people an opportunity to reap. Yes, there will always be those who will be resistant when it comes to sowing seed. But what I am saying is the anointing on your life should speak for itself. If you are good ground, the results of the anointing to remove burdens and destroy yokes, will command money to be attracted to you. People will give their last because they are grateful for what God has done through you. The anointing will cause people to give to you.

Give, and it shall be given unto you; good measure, pressed down, and shaken together, and running over, shall men give into your bosom. For with the same measure that ye mete withal it shall be measured to you again. (Luke 6:38)

I think we as ministers particularly, have allowed the spirit of familiarity to actually rob us from this scripture manifesting overflow in our lives. When this scripture comes "alive" in your life it will cause an overflow of abundance to manifest continuously. So many times I hear ministers say that they are living in the overflow but yet there is no divine manifestation. When you are living in the overflow signs and wonders will follow. In order for an overflow to manifest you first must be full. There is a realm that you can walk and live in where your countenance says, "I attract money."

Conclusion

There is an anointing for prosperity, for giving and for reaping. When there is an anointing for reaping, there will be a divine manifestation of prosperity and money and it will show up in your life. It will flood and overflow in your life, just as you pour water into a glass and when that glass gets full it will start to flood over. As long as the water is steady running, it will cause a continuous overflow; which represents the open windows of heaven pouring out a blessing. When there is not room enough to receive, it will cause a divine manifestation and overflow of money being loosed in your life.

APPENDIX A

Kim's Money Confession

I declare that I am a money magnet.
I command my money to be loosed in the earth daily therefore the heavens must loose my money daily.
I decree and declare that money is being loosed right now from the heavens.
When I call money it comes.
Money I call you right now, I command you to come to me right now, I summon you and I decree that you will obey.
I talk to money and I say Money I control you, you will never control me therefore money you must obey me now.
Everywhere I go the manifestation of money shows up in my life because I attract money, I never chase money.
Money hunts me down, it looks for me, money knows how to find me and it finds me daily.
Goodness and mercy follows after me all the days of my life.
Money follows and chases after me everywhere I go.
Every day there is a divine manifestation of money in my bank accounts.
My bank accounts are filled with thousands of dollars daily.
I make money every day.
I call money to my bank accounts right now.
Money I command you to manifest yourself.
I am anointed to reap therefore I reap what I sow and I sow money because I am a seed sower therefore money comes back to me and Men give to my life daily; good measure, pressed down, shaken together and running over.

The windows of heaven are wide open to me pouring out a blessing that there will not be room enough to receive causing an overflow of the blessing in my life.
Money overflows in my personal life, business and bank accounts.
Money is flowing in me like a river right now, it never stops flowing.
I have the ability and power to produce as much money as I desire whenever I get ready because the source of money lives in me.
Ideas, insight and concepts from the heavens come to me daily to produce millions.
Millionaire status is in my DNA, it abides and dwells in me.
I produce millions of dollars daily because I am a money maker.
When people come in contact with me they come in contact with money.
I am known all around the World as "The God Made Millionaire" and People call me Kim K. Sanders (replace with your name) the Money Maker.
I am fruitful and I multiply like My God, producing continuously after my own kind therefore I produce other millionaires.
I reproduce my success into my children and into the lives of those that sit before me.
I decree and I declare that I will never in my life be broke.
I detest poverty and I am allergic to being broke.
I decree that anything broke that comes into my presence must be fixed because I am a money maker; I make, construct, build and produce money makers.
I make money come into existence and into my presence with my seeds and my words, because I have been given the power to get wealth.
God is the author of money, He has written the book, and He has given me the manuscript and the copyright to publish it publicly in my life.
Money rains on me.
Money overwhelms me, it overtakes me.

Loose Your Money – Make Money Obey You

I am saturated with money, from the top of my head to the soles of my feet.
I make money while I am sleeping.
Money is making its way to me right now.
When I talk to money, money listens so money you must obey because I have authority over you, therefore I command you to be loosed from the heavens.
I am a money attracter.
Money comes to me unhindered.
Money flows to me like a river a constant steady flow.
Money finds me daily. It comes into my presence.
I produce hidden treasures of secret places.
There is not a day that goes by that I don't make money.
Money comes to me from hidden places.
I receive money right now.
My countenance says money. When people look at me they see money. When people come into my presence they give to me.
My countenance demands that people sow into my life.
Everywhere I go I run into money.
Money obeys me quickly as fast as I call it, money comes.

APPENDIX B

Kim's Prosperity Confession

I am prosperous.
Prosperity is who I am.
It belongs to me.
It is in my DNA.
When people see me, they see prosperity because I am prosperity.
I am prosperous in all that I do.
Everything I put my hands to, it prospers because prosperity lives in me.
It abides in me.
It dwells in me.
It overflows in me because I fill myself with prosperity food.
I have a prosperous mind, soul, and body.
I live a prosperous life, because I represent God in the earth.
God is prosperity, therefore I am prosperity.
Total life prosperity is my portion.
God has given me the power to get wealth.
Therefore, I have the ability, the endowment and power to have wealth.
The prosperity anointing is flowing in my life.
Everything I do and touch prospers.
I am clothed in prosperity.
And prosperity looks good on me.
Prosperity saturates my mind and soul
I think prosperous thoughts daily
I am subject to the spirit of prosperity only, therefore, I refuse, reject, resist poverty; and I am allergic to being broke.
I have a prosperity vocabulary, which causes me to have a prosperous mouth.

Loose Your Money – Make Money Obey You

I speak prosperity to my spirit, soul, and body.
I speak prosperity to my business, therefore, my clients and customers are prospering.
I speak prosperity to my bank accounts, therefore I decree and declare that there will be a divine manifestation of money in my bank accounts today because prosperity belongs to me. It is a part of my covenant.
I say that I have prosperous relationships, starting with my family.
My family is prosperous.
My children are prosperous.
And prosperity lives and abides in my home.
Prosperity rests in my atmosphere.
Everywhere I go, I prosper.
I deposit prosperity into the lives of others.
I am a prosperity guru.
I produce prosperity.
When people look at me, they see prosperity.
Prosperity recognizes me everywhere I go.
Prosperity is subject to me.
My name (put your name in it) is associated with prosperity.
I represent prosperity, riches, and wealth in the earth.
When people hear my name, they think prosperity.
When people see me, they say, (put our name) is prosperous.
I draw prosperity to me
I attract prosperity to me
And I associate with prosperity only.
I was born to be prosperous and my whole life represents total life prosperity in the earth.

ABOUT THE AUTHOR

Kim K. Sanders is the founder of Kim K. Sanders International, LLC and the founder of Kim K. Sanders Ministries Inc. Kim is an Author, Ordained Prophet, Breakthrough Life Coach, Mentor and Entrepreneur. As a personal development expert, Kim trains aspiring leaders and conscious entrepreneurs, who desire to embrace excellence and produce authentic breakthrough results. Kim teaches practical and spiritual principles to acquire and maintain extraordinary wealth, health and relationships. Kim's mission is to provoke people to pay the price to pursue their passions to produce power, profits and total life prosperity on purpose. She uses her 25 years of experience to strategically help individuals refocus, reshape, reposition and realign their lives to fulfill their divine purposes and live maximized lives.

Kim is an online media personality known for her direct and bold in-your-face approach that has transformed lives all around the World with a global reach of the USA all the way to Russia. Her internet marketing expertise was developed from building a unique authentic brand online by leveraging social media and video marketing. Many of Kim's clients and protégés attribute their personal accomplishments to her ability to identify the source of the problem and get to the solution.

Kim's Online Classes and Live Training Events will change the Life of ANYONE who sits under the sound of Her Voice! Some of Kim's Trainings include: "Love Yourself To Life" "Walk in Your Authentic Divine Purpose" "Positioning Yourself For Wealth," "How To Attract Money" and "Loose Your Money."

Loose Your Money – Make Money Obey You

Being blessed to live an above average lifestyle, it is the Lord who empowers Kim to prosper and He takes pleasure in her prosperity according to Deuteronomy 8:18 and Psalms 35:27.

To host the *"Loose Your Money Conference"* or request Kim K. Sanders to come to your City visit: www.kimksanders.com or call 888-664-8881.

www.ingramcontent.com/pod-product-compliance
Lightning Source LLC
Chambersburg PA
CBHW070631300426
44113CB00010B/1736